The Five-Minute Miracle

BOOKS BY ED DELPH

Learning How To Trust Again
The Five-Minute Miracle

AVAILABLE FROM DESTINY IMAGE PUBLISHERS

The Five-Minute Miracle

Standing Out by Becoming Outstanding

Ed Delph

DESTINY IMAGE® PUBLISHERS, INC.

P.O. Box 310, Shippensburg, PA 17257-0310

"Speaking to the Purposes of God for this Generation and for the Generations to Come."

This book and all other Destiny Image, Revival Press, Mercy Place, Fresh Bread, Destiny Image Fiction, and Treasure House books are available at Christian bookstores and distributors worldwide.

For a U.S. bookstore nearest you, call **1-800-722-6774**.

For more information on foreign distributors, call **717-532-3040**.

Reach us on the Internet at **www.destinyimage.com**.

ISBN 10: 0-7684-2765-7

ISBN 13: 978-0-7684-2765-3

For Worldwide Distribution, Printed in the U.S.A.

1 2 3 4 5 6 7 8 9 10 11 /11 10 09 08

Dedication

This book is dedicated to Canada and the United States, two great countries whose leadership, core values, and ideals have influenced all the nations of the world.

Acknowledgments

This book has so many stories and one-liners that mentioning everyone would be impossible. I have made an honest effort to recognize all sources. I love to make other people known!

I am grateful to an English quarterly publication, *The Word For Today*,[1] that has many excellent examples and stories. I want to thank author Laurie Beth Jones for her book *Teach Your Team To Fish*,[2] and for her creativity and love for people. I thank author Mike Murdock for his two books *Wisdom for Crisis Times*[3] and *The One-Minute Businessman's Devotional*.[4] Ideas are plentiful in his books.

I used one or two ideas and stories from author Zig Ziglar's book, *Life Lifters*.[5] Also, author Dwight Thompson for his book, *Power Principles For Power Living*.[6]

Many jokes in this book were taken from the Website cybersalt.org/cleanlaugh.[7] Thank you Pastor Tim Davis for your ministry!

I thank my wife, Becky, who does the primary editing on the articles and makes sure that they are ready to send out to all our publishers and friends. Couldn't do it without you, Beckers!

Thanks also to Carolyn Dryer, editor of *The Glendale Star* and *The Peoria Times*, who produces excellent newspapers for the Glendale and Peoria communities. You are wonderful! Also, Bill Toops, publisher of the *Star* and *Times*, for giving me the opportunity to write and redefine in the public arena which makes our community better. Thank you for building our community through a media that report the news, and don't make the news.

Thanks to Steve Lingenfelter, pastor of New Life Church in Peoria, Arizona, who challenged me to write this book. His heart is for people in the community and it shows in everything he does. What an example to me!

Endorsements

As a pastor who has for many years embraced the mission of connecting the *message* of the church with the *audience* of the community, I heartily recommend to you this book. Ed's entertaining and creative style of writing from God's perspective on everyday issues is certain to inspire, refresh, and motivate the whole community—and that's a good thing!

—Walther P. Kallestad, Senior Pastor
Community Church of Joy, Peoria, Arizona

In a world of fast-paced, sound-bite, media-driven info-living, Ed Delph brings the reality of God, the Church, and Christians to the 90 percent of us who have only 10 percent of our time to focus on these weighty matters. Yet he does it in a way that allows us to take bite-sized nuggets of the depths of God's ancient truth. You will find yourself "holding a smile" as you read the witty passages, while being subtly and profoundly reminded of the eternal wisdom of a personal encounter with God—not framed by reality television, but by relationship with the Almighty. Thanks Ed, for reminding us—not only the media and those outside the church, but Christians as well—of who we are intended to be.

—Dr. Jannah Scott, currently on assignment as
Policy Advisor, Faith & Community Initiatives
Office of the Governor, Arizona

Ed Delph's new book would make a great gift for your employees and business associates. It shares the Good News of a Christian lifestyle in a punchy, easy-to-read style. You will enjoy reading it and sharing it with others!

—Ralph Palmen, President
Pinnacle Forum America

Ed Delph reveals that the Church is the world in obedience to Christ. He addresses the mass of humanity who are legally released from Adam's inferior reference given to man to Christ's triumph as every human's inheritance given freely by grace. This book is a mindskin worth pouring your thoughts into.

—Alan Platt
Visionary Leader: Doxa Deo
Pretoria, South Africa

Ed Delph has blessed the Body of Christ with wisdom to communicate the Gospel to people in a very effective way. The Holy Sprit is pressing the Church to be reformed in its thinking and ways to bring transformation to communities, cities, and nations. Thanks Ed, for showing a way to fulfill our commission to bring transformation by taking the Kingdom of God into the kingdom of media and all other kingdoms of this world. Your life, ministry, and wisdom from God have greatly blessed us.

—Dr. Bill Hamon, Bishop
Founder, Christian International Ministries Network
Author, *Prophets and Personal Prophecy,*
Day of the Saints, and many others

Ed Delph's book is an important contribution at a critical time. Through the media, families are exposed daily to drugs, abuse, and violence with little or no understanding of God and His Word. Citizens tolerate abusive behavior in homes, schools, and neighborhoods. Ed's book is a wake-up call to understand the power of God in our lives. With understanding comes change as individuals create spiritually healthy families and communities.

—Stephanie L. Mann, crime and violence prevention consultant
San Francisco, California
www.stephanielmann.com

Ed Delph's stance that God has received a bad rap in the media prompted him to action. Fighting fire with fire, he uses that very same media to turn the tables. His newspaper columns shout out the news—contrary to what you may have heard, God is alive and well and living among us. Ed's contemporary method of setting the record straight beckons us to see God's power as He moves in our everyday lives.

—Cathy Carlat, Vice Mayor
City of Peoria, Arizona

Ed Delph has a unique way of presenting complex ideas in simple ways that the reader can understand and remember. In this new book, Ed brings the concepts of biblical knowledge into modern relevance and understanding. This book is great for everyone wanting to see God at work in our everyday lives and especially for pastors who are leading congregations in the 21st century. You will come away inspired after reading this book.

—Greg Brown, Senior Pastor
Skyway Church

Thank you, Ed Delph, for an easy read and much-needed answer to the misinformation and attacks on God's masterpiece, the 21st-century Church. It should be read by saint and sinner alike. What would the world be like without the real, relevant Church? Jesus said the Church is the salt and light to transform the universe.

—Apostle Emanuele Cannistraci
Founder, Apostolic Missions International

The words that God gave to you sparked life into me, Ed. You are a voice God uses to bring direction to the Body of Christ. Thank you for your faithfulness.

—Tim Hampton, Commander
Maryvale Precinct
Phoenix Police Department

Ed Delph is one of the premier thinkers in the world today regarding the Church's mission to serve communities and connect people to God. His unique ability to convey timeless truths through wit and humor is a breath of fresh air to those who are hungry for God but weary of dead religion.

—Joseph Mattera
Resurrection Church of New York
Brooklyn, New York

Ed Delph is a Christian missions practitioner. I know of no one like him who can make something complex sound simple. It was Albert Einstein who said, "If you can't explain it simply, you don't understand it well enough." This book will be essential reading for everyone who takes seriously the heart of God for the people who live around them. Like his previous books, Ed provides the handles we need to grab a good hold of the things that are important.

—Brian Medway
Life Purpose, Australia

Ed Delph is the real deal. He has great insights—and a deep passion for God's people to make a Kingdom difference in our world. God is using him worldwide. Let God use him to speak to you in this great book!

—Dr. Gary D. Kinnaman, Author, Activist
Pastor at Large, City of Grace
Mesa, Arizona

This book will be a blessing to you because Ed Delph is a blessing. He knows how to make words come alive, and make you think about things you never thought of before. As you read, don't hear what he didn't say, hear what he is saying.

—Pastor Francis Armstrong
Third Day Worship Centre
Kingston, Ontario, Canada

Ed's statement that "Perception is reality to the uninformed," is a reflection of the real challenge we face. I think Ed has once again given the Body of Christ a resource tool to address this issue. This book can be used as an evangelistic tool, a daily Bible study, or a study of the philosophies of a church-community connection. This book will not only inspire all who read it, but will increase the effectiveness of any church culture and help change the uninformed world perception of the Christian church. Ed clearly brings the spiritual truths to a practical reality!

—Gary W. Carter, Pastor
Drayton Valley Word of Life Church
Drayton Valley, Alberta, Canada

Those who know Ed Delph knows he is at home and at his very best when he is connecting God to the community. For many "old timers" it is often painful to be confronted with the increasing irreligious and post-Christian mindset of many people in First World countries. Ed Delph has the experience and God-given ability to bridge this gap.

—Dr. Isak Burger, President
Apostolic Faith Mission
South Africa

Every now and then God gives a simple truth to a writer which opens the gates of the mind to revelation. This is one of those truths. Every believer should carry this book as an important tool for evangelism. It answers most of the questions of the unbeliever and stirs the faith of the believer to realize that what we need is on the shelf of God's storehouse for the taking.

Thanks to Ed Delph we now have a concise and clear understanding of why we are here, and of God's expectations of us. No religious jargon from this writer; he tells it as it is. God has no favorites and excludes no one from partaking of abundant living. You cannot read this book and remain a doubter of God.

—Iverna Tompkins
Iverna Tompkins Ministries

This book is a great easy read. The chapters are a mixture of timeless truths and humorous insights—a great book to add to your own reading, and a helpful resource for someone searching for truth.

—Luke Brough, National Leader
Elim Churches of New Zealand

This is the book I needed as pastor of a congregation for "people who don't like church." It is a tool to equip and empower followers of Christ to reach out to their neighbors and neighborhoods. We need more how-to-think-rightly instruction before we break the holy huddle to act righteously up and down the streets of our cities and communities.

—Phil Miglioratti
Loving Our Communities to Christ
www.missionamerica.org

The genius of this book must have come from God Himself. What a wonderful tool. This book is needed more today than ever before. We live in a generation with a very tainted image of God; so thank you, Ed, for being willing and available to place a straight stick against a crooked one, and helping others know and understand the genuine love and goodness of God.

—Trevor Yaxley
Trustee/Director, Lifeway Trust
For Success…For Life, www.lifeway.ac.nz
Huhu Studios, "Animation with Character," www.huhustudios.com

Ed communicates his passion to see the Church active and effective in the community with such relevance that it puts things in the grasp of all who read it—regardless of race, gender, or creed—it cross all barriers. His contemporary thinking comes to life, making this a practical teaching relevant to our spiritual growth.

—Ps. Kindah Greening
King's Christian Group, Gold Coast, Australia

Contents

Foreword

There are few things quite as boring as being religious, and nothing more exciting as being in a growing relationship with God! A search to discover God, to some, can seem like nothing more than just fulfilling some religious obligation that relieves their conscious—for the moment. But for those who truly find God, life is never the same. A life of discovering God is full of rich experiences.

In a fast-changing 21st-century world, it can seem as if the Bible and our understanding of God are ancient and not applicable to our daily lives. That couldn't be further from the truth! The everlasting qualities of God and His unwavering love for us continue to this day.

Jesus said, "I have come that they may have life, and have it to the full" (John 10:10). Most people are working to try to create a great life. The reality is that their path is wrought with failure. They are like cars without gas, pens without ink, and become exhausted by their own effort. Humankind was created by God so that the presence of the Creator could produce life—real life—through humanity. Christ gave Himself for us to give Himself to us!

I have found Ed Delph particularly gifted in communicating these truths in our modern context. We are living in an age when proclamation cannot stand without demonstration. There is nothing more powerful than seeing God work through a person's life—except being that person! This book is inspirational to the one who is on a journey to find God, as well as those who have already found Him.

Ed shares many real-life stories that demonstrate the power of God's Word when it is applied to our everyday circumstances. Ed's simple approach and pithy statements capture our imagination of what could be. This book is a "no nonsense book" that takes life head-on. You'll find it full of spiritual insight and common sense, enjoyable, and easy to read.

—Steve Lingenfelter, Senior Pastor
New Life Church, Peoria, Arizona

Preface

What if what you have heard about God is not entirely true?

What if what you heard about churches is not entirely true?

What if what you heard about Christians is not entirely true?

What if you have formed your opinions about God, church, and Christians based on only a small part of the big picture?

What if you formed a strategy of living based on partial truths and partial untruths about God, church, and Christians?

What if you formed your belief system and life outlook on someone else's agenda-driven opinions on what God, church, and Christians are like, rather than forming your own opinions?

What are most churches and church people really like, and why do they think the way they do?

What is God really like?

Is God just for the uneducated and unaware to believe in?

Is God a Republican?

Is God the One who causes wars?

Are all churches after your money, or only a few?

Are all Christians weird, or just a few?

If God were to speak in your language to your real-life issues, what do you think He would say?

What if we could clear away the static of other opinions, tune into God, and find out what He thinks about you and your everyday life?

Do you think you can learn about Him and end up not being "religious" and all that other stuff?

In other words, *can you know and trust God totally with your life?*

Some Answers

Good questions, huh? If you are looking for answers to some of these questions, there is a good chance that you will find them in this book.

This book is for two types of people. The first type includes those who may have never considered God—or may be open to the idea of God, but are not sure what to believe about God, church, and Christians. With so many ideas and opinions out there, it's hard to know what to believe, isn't it? And everyone can point out an example, can't they? Everyone has a plan for your life. Everyone wants your vote. Everyone wants you to believe as they do. It seems as if everyone has their own agenda, don't they?

The second type includes the churched people who are looking for real-life answers to everyday issues. This book equips you for life, not just church life. It's wisdom for everyday living. I address issues that you may never hear spoken about in your church. Churches are generally very good at churchy stuff, but not always the best at real-life stuff. Most seminaries don't always equip pastors for those issues either.

So I have written on everyday issues, on everyday things, in everyday language that you, your friends, your family, and your community will understand. It's theologically correct yet totally relatable. There's no compromise, but there is courtesy. It has the best meat of all for churched people...wisdom!

Everyone loves to laugh and you will laugh. The purpose of this book is to build a bridge between you, the reader, and God. I desire to help you find God, humorously and tactfully. Someone once said, "Tact is the art of making a point without making an enemy." That is what I do. I tell the truth, and I use wisdom. At the very least, you will get another opinion.

The chapters are bite-size (and very nutritious!), so you can read one or a few at work, at play, at home, in the bathroom, wherever. They aren't lengthy discourses weighted down with terms impossible to digest. The topics will inspire, encourage, motivate, and get your day going. The topics are enjoyable and engaging, yet impacting and transforming. You will discover the real God by finding out what He thinks about your everyday issues.

I share with you some of the things I have learned about God as a pastor since 1980, a Doctor of Ministry, businessman, educator, and as a newspaper writer. I hope to add to all those other opinions of God that you have heard. I hope to give you a more complete and accurate picture of God. Perhaps I can move you from unaware to aware, from uninterested to interested, from unconcerned to concerned, or maybe even from antagonistic toward God to accepting His love. I hope to open hearts, open minds, and open doors for God to have influence in your life.

For churched people, this book is a great resource to grow in the grace and knowledge of our Lord. It's also a wonderful resource to give to your friends, family, neighbors, coworkers, and the community to introduce them through practical wisdom to the God who loves them. To our friends who are un-churched, please read and enjoy. I promise we will be friends afterward—and you will be equipped for a more meaningful and productive life, if nothing else but by the wisdom of God.

So clear the static, open your mind, and enjoy the revelation. Allow God to speak through the words you read. Enjoy it and employ it! You aren't "spending time" reading this book, you are "investing time," and you will get a great return on your investment!

Introduction

Redefining God in a 21st-Century World

"The most important thing in communications is to hear what isn't being said."
—Peter Drucker[8]

Two major television networks conducted polls on the following questions: "Should the motto 'In God We Trust' be removed from U.S. currency?" The other: "Should the words 'under God' be removed from the Pledge of Allegiance?" It was reported that these two polls had the highest number of responses ever recorded. The results: 80 percent of those who responded voted to keep the words "In God We Trust," and 85 percent voted to keep "under God" in the Pledge of Allegiance. That is a significant commanding public response![9]

People *are* interested in God, but there is a problem. Those who are interested in knowing more about God are not quite sure who God is. Today's media, academia, government, and other institutions portray God as something (not Someone) from yesterday, not today. God comes across as something superstitious and old fashioned—something for those who are not "enlightened" to believe in and depend on. These days, God comes across as uninvolved in the affairs of humankind. God comes across, well, as dead or missing in action.

Besides that, it seems like churches and Christians don't even know what they believe. Headlines are full of this pastor's affair, that church person murdering a spouse, or some church going "out of business" leaving many bills unpaid. Add to those negative scenarios, the culture of some churches and church people who are disconnected from and condescending to the community—no wonder unchurched people are confused. Because of problems like these and the way they are reported, the church has one of the poorest public relations images, especially with those who are between 16-29 years of age in North America. Of course, these types of failures are blamed on God, and as a result, many great people who might be interested in God get turned off.[10] Perception is reality.

The Bell-Shaped Curve

Think about this. Most everything in life can be described as a bell-shaped curve concept: the greatest number of representations will be in the middle of the curve. That is the area where most people are, most churches are, most lifestyles are, etc. As you go toward the outer edges of the bell curve, the number of normal distribution instances decrease significantly. With that idea in mind, from a national media ratings perspective, does "common" create high viewer ratings, or do "extremes" generate higher viewer ratings?

We love extremes, don't we? We love to read stories that stimulate us. Extremes are like gossip, bigger than life. Extremes have the effect of making us think that all movie stars are _____, all politicians are _____, or all pastors and churches are _____. Media and communication entities effectively normalize the abnormal and visa versa. Today, the ends of the bell-shaped curve seem like the middle. The extremes have replaced the normal, making the abnormal seem normal.

National media focus on the extreme examples in business, politics, organizations, and the people involved—because that is where the high ratings are. Just watch any of the reality shows or entertainment news. We have all been influenced by this constant focus on extremism. What we see and read forms our opinions and influences how we act and what we think. We must remember that extremism is not a reflection of the majority of people or institutions in our nation. Only a very small percentage of what the national media focuses on becomes larger than life. Unfortunately, though, perception becomes reality for some. Opinions are formed, decisions are made, and public relations images are created—all based on media hype. It's quite a problem and most all of us have been influenced by this phenomenon.

This has especially affected what people think about God, church, and Christians. National media report the failures, the extremes, the bad moments, and the worst examples. While these stories may be true, what about the 95 percent of pastors, churches, and churched people who are living out their relationship with God with grace and goodness?

The Entire Picture

What about the large majority of pastors who have served their communities and given their entire lives to helping others? What about the large majority of local church members who have been pillars in the community for many years? What about the millions of Christians who are walking daily with God in a very real way? What about the middle of the bell-shaped curve? Yes it's easy to report the extreme, and yes there are bad examples in every institution, but is it fair to label all because of a few? Is it fair to label God as incompetent or not relevant because of a few extreme and inaccurate examples?

It is impossible to describe an elephant if you only see his trunk. You would be partially correct, but not fully correct, which could mislead many in what an elephant actually looks like.

In the same respect, it is impossible to describe God, church, and Christians if you only partially see (or read about) Him and some of His children. Public relationships of all kinds of people and institutions have been ruined by not seeing the entire picture. Media are notorious for presenting extremes. Peter Drucker's quote at the beginning of this chapter states what

I'm saying perfectly: "The most important thing in communication is to hear what isn't being said." That's true literally and intellectually!

Opening Hearts, Minds, and Doors

In November 2004, I was so concerned about the public relations image of God, church, and Christians, that I made a decision that would change my life. I decided to take steps to improve God's public image. My friends, family, and the community that I serve were being influenced by a perception of the church that was really not the reality of the church at all.

I decided that if I was going to change the public's perception of God, church, and Christians, I was going to have to be part of media. I was going to have to try and change the image of the church from the inside out, not the outside in. I figured that my definition of God, church, and Christians was more informed than the national media's definition, because I can personally describe the entire picture—not just the trunk!

I met with the publisher and owner of Pueblo Publishers which publishes two local weekly paid subscription newspapers, *The Glendale Star* and *The Peoria Times*. I expressed to him my concern with mainline media's tendency to report the extremes and how this was hindering our community and churches and deliberately concealing the contributions of God. Bill Toops challenged me to write a weekly article for *The Star* and *Times* that would allow me to redefine some of the public's perceptions about God, church, and Christians. I agreed, if the column would be titled "The Church-Community Connection."

The idea was to open hearts, minds, and doors for God in our community. I live in a suburb of Phoenix, Arizona, called Peoria, and I wanted our community to have a positive experience with God through my articles. I am now actively redefining God and pastoring approximately 100,000 people weekly in the community through my articles. People are receiving a truer definition of God, church, and Christians. The response from the community has been fantastic. Thanks to God, I am quite a celebrity around our community. Other newspapers are also publishing my articles.

That is what brings me to this book. Each chapter is an article that I wrote for *The Glendale Star* and *The Peoria Times*. The chapters are relevant, humorous, creative, empowering, and manageable. God is speaking to us today about everyday issues in everyday language. He is the God you can know by what He has to say on matters that you are interested in. He wants only the best for you.

1

What You Could Do If...

What you could do if you didn't know you couldn't—I love that concept! Zig Ziglar uses that concept in one of the chapters in his book, *Life Lifters*.[11]

One day I was in Resistencia, Argentina, watching a fisherman catch dorado. The fish are so big—up to four or five feet—that ocean fishing gear is required. The fisherman threw out his line and soon he had a big dorado on the line. It took 20 minutes to pull the fish in, but he finally got it to shore. I thought, *That dorado is going to be on the asado [grill] tonight!* But no, he threw it back in the water.

He went fishing again. This time he caught a bigger dorado. It took him 25 minutes to pull it in. I thought, *That dorado is going to be on the asado tonight!* But just like the last time, he threw the fish back in the water. I was stunned.

He went fishing again. This time he caught a tiny little dorado. To my surprise, he kept it! The next time he caught the biggest dorado of all. It was about 5 feet long. It took him 30 minutes to pull it in. He got it on shore, then threw it back in the river.

Finally I asked him in my best Spanish why he was keeping the small fish and throwing back the large.

His reply, "I only have a ten-inch frying pan!"

Many people think that way. They limit what they can do because they don't know they can do it. The fisherman's "mindskin," was too small—he could have cut the first big fish into smaller pieces and cooked it a little at a time. It takes a new, larger way of perceiving life to create a more successful life.

Most of us were designed to catch big fish. But it's hard to fit a 16-by-20 idea into a 3-by-5 mindset. Most all of us were created to have a 5-foot frying pan, designed to hold big fish. It's not a matter of capacity. It's a matter of competency and motivation—especially motivation. That God-part of us is waiting to be released.

How do you do what you don't know you can do? Never think or speak negatively about yourself. That puts you in disagreement with God. Meditate on your God-given strengths, and learn to encourage yourself, for much of the time nobody else will. Focus on your potential, not your limitations. Remember, God lives in you through Christ. Have the courage to be different, Jesus was. Learn to handle criticism. Let it develop you, not discourage you. **Determine your own worth instead of letting others do it for you. They will shortchange you almost every time!**

Be a player in life, not just a spectator. When you go the extra mile, you are seldom in a traffic jam. You can do all things God wants you to do though Christ who strengthens you.

Now, *that's* a big frying pan!

••

Enlarge your mindset by:

Not thinking or speaking negatively about yourself.
Meditating on your God-given strengths and encouraging yourself.
Focusing on your potential.
Determining your own worth.
Knowing that you can do all things through Christ.

2

Being a Good Finder

Through the years I have watched our culture slowly but surely shift to finding the negative first, and the positive second. In this day of micromanaging, bloggers, and accusations, it is hard to find anything positive. Even if you point out something positive, you are accused of having your head in the sand. My advice, don't be a fault finder, be a good finder.

The story is told of a king in Africa who had a close friend with whom he grew up. The friend had a habit of looking at every situation that ever occurred in his life (positive or negative) and remarking, "This is good!" One day the king and his friend were on a hunting expedition. The friend loaded and prepared the guns for the king. The friend had apparently done something wrong in preparing one of the guns, for after taking the gun from his friend, the king fired it and his thumb was blown off. Examining the situation, the friend remarked as usual, "This is good!" To which the king replied, "No, this is not good!" and proceeded to send his friend to jail.

About a year later, the king was hunting in an area that he should have known to stay clear of. Cannibals captured him and took him to their village. They tied him, stacked some wood, set up a stake, and bound him to it. As they came near to set fire to the wood, they noticed that the king was missing a thumb. Being superstitious, they never ate anyone who was less than whole. So untying the king, they sent him on his way. As he returned home, he was reminded of the event that had taken his thumb, and felt remorse for the treatment of his friend.

He went immediately to the jail. "You were right," he said, "it was good that my thumb was blown off." He proceeded to tell the friend all that had happened. "And so, I am sorry for sending you to jail for so long. It was wrong of me to do this."

"No," his friend replied, "This is good!"

"What do you mean, 'this is good?' How could it be good that I sent my friend to jail for a year?"

His friend replied, "If I had not been in jail, I would have been with you!"[12]

Maybe it's time to start looking for positive news in the midst of all the negative.

Some people find fault like there's a reward for it. Don't be a fault finder, be a good finder.

••

Be a finder of good news. Look for the good world leaders, national officials, state administrators, community managers, church leaders, family, and friends. Then pass on the good news...especially the Good News of Jesus Christ.

3

Shake It Off and Step Up

I'm sure you noticed by now that life has its up's and down's. Some days you are the dog, other days you are the hydrant! Ever feel that way? I have. There's a story that has brought me perspective and encouragement during those hydrant days. It was sent to me years ago by a friend who is an Air Force officer.

A parable is told of a farmer who owned an old mule. The mule fell into the farmer's well. The farmer heard the mule braying, or whatever mules do when they fall into wells. After carefully assessing the situation, the farmer sympathized with the mule, but decided that neither the mule nor the well was worth the trouble of saving.

Instead, he called his neighbors together and told them what had happened. He enlisted them to haul dirt to bury the old mule in the well and put him out of his misery.

Initially, the old mule was hysterical. But as the farmer and his neighbors continued shoveling the dirt on his back a thought dawned on him—every time a shovelful of dirt landed on his back he should shake it off and step up. This he did, blow after blow. He kept saying to himself, *shake it off and step up…shake it off and step up…shake it off and step up*!

No matter how painful the blows. No matter how distressing the situation. The old mule fought panic, fear, and self-pity. He just kept shaking it off and stepping up. Yup. It wasn't long before the old mule, battered and exhausted, stepped triumphantly over the wall of that well.

What may have buried him, actually blessed him. Why? Because of the way he handled adversity.

Perhaps the challenges and adversities we face also have the potential of benefit and blessing. The outcome depends on the way we respond to our problems. Kites fly highest when facing into a big wind.

Sir Edmund Hillary, the first person to climb Mount Everest, sums it all up after he failed in his first attempt to climb the mountain. As he was descending the mountain, he suddenly turned, looked up and spoke to "his" mountain saying, "You defeated me! But you won't defeat me again! Because you have grown all you can grow...but I haven't."[13]

Perhaps we can learn from Sir Edmund Hillary and an old mule the next time we have a hydrant day...shake it off and step up!

∙∙∙

Facing difficult circumstances can be rough—but knowing that God has provided a solution for every problem is reassuring. Check out His Word—the answers are all there.

And who of you by being worried can add a single hour to his life? And why are you worried about clothing? Observe how the lilies of the field grow; they do not toil nor do they spin, yet I say to you that not even Solomon in all his glory clothed himself like one of these. But if God so clothes the grass of the field, which is alive today and tomorrow is thrown into the furnace, will He not much more clothe you? (Matthew 6:27-30)

4

Be Careful What You Ask For

A couple had been married for 40 years and also celebrated their 60th birthdays. During the celebration, a fairy appeared and said that because they had been such a loving couple all those years, she would give them each one wish. The wife wanted to travel around the world. The fairy waved her wand and boom…she had tickets in her hand. Next, it was the husband's turn. He paused briefly for a moment and then said shyly, "Well, I'd like to have a woman 30 years younger than me." The fairy picked up her wand and boom…he was 90!

The woman said, "Amen!"

Believe it or not, there is a lesson to be learned from this story—be careful what you ask for. I'm not saying that you shouldn't ask God, I'm saying to be careful what you ask for.

I love the story of Solomon in the Bible in First Kings chapter 3. God appeared to Solomon in a dream and said, "Ask what you wish me to give you." Solomon could have asked for anything! He could have asked for riches, a long life, revenge on his enemies, the latest chariot with all the bells and whistles. Why, he could have asked to be on the front page of all those magazines at the grocery store check-out counter!

What did Solomon ask of God? "So give Your servant an understanding heart to judge Your people to discern between good and evil. For who is able to judge this great people of Yours?" (1 Kings 3:9).

Solomon asked for wisdom, understanding, and character—for the sake of the people and the community. I think that request woke up angels in Heaven! I can hear Gabriel saying to Michael. "Did you hear that? He didn't want fame, fortune, or frolic!"

Solomon could handle a promotion because he thought of others first. Too many these days ask for themselves first. It's all about *them*—just like the man who wanted a woman 30 years younger.

How did God respond to Solomon? "Behold, I have done according to your words...I have given you a wise and discerning heart...and...I have also given you what you have not asked, both riches and honor, so that there will not be any among the kings like you all of your days" (1 Kings 3:12-13).

God answers our requests three ways: "Yes," "No," and "You've got to be kidding!"

Seek first the Kingdom of God and all these things will be added unto you (Matt. 6:33). Aim at earth and you get nothing, aim at Heaven and you get earth thrown in!

Remember, be careful what you ask for!

....

Therefore I say to you, all things for which you pray and ask, believe that you have received them, and they will be granted you (Mark 11:24).

...From everyone who has been given much, much will be required; and to whom they entrusted much, of him they will ask all the more (Luke 12:48).

Until now you have asked for nothing in My name; ask and you will receive, so that your joy may be made full (John 16:24).

5

Richly Blessed, Deeply Loved, and Highly Favored

As I travel the globe speaking at leadership conferences, every once and awhile I meet someone who brings special refreshment, a beyond-the-borders approach to Christianity, and a profound but simple wisdom. Such was the case when I met Jimmy Lim in Singapore. Simply said, he is a character that has *character*!

Jimmy was my host on a trip to Singapore. I stayed at his home, ate sensational Chinese food prepared by his wife, Christine, and his Indonesian household attendant. During our time together, Jimmy gave me his philosophy of life and Christianity. I was in Singapore at the invitation of Vicar Tan Piah of St. Hilda's Anglican Church. His invitation was wonderfully Chinese…"Whatever you are doing in February, you will cancel because you are coming to Singapore." How could I resist?

Jimmy Lim, a retired businessman, loves to serve the Lord by serving the church. Frankly, with his business skills, he could run St. Hilda's church, but would rather help people, the pastor, and be a "servant for the Lord." That's what it's all about, isn't it?

However, Jimmy, being an entrepreneur at heart, began thinking, *What can I do to make some extra spending money.* Jimmy said that God gave him an idea—parrots! He bought two African gray parrots. "Then I rememba Bible verse that say…be frueful and multiply. I speak to birds…Be frueful and multiply." Sure enough, not long afterward there were four eggs in the parrots'

41

nest. Just like I couldn't say "No" to Tan Piah, the parrots could not say no to Jimmy armed with the Word of God! Now he has 12 breeding pairs, African Grays and Yellow Amazons that "be frueful and multiply." Jimmy says that the birds obey the Word of God! He sells them for about $500 U.S. each.

"I want to work at church…vedy eye opening experience. Sometimes Christian like Chinese proverb…the tiger's head…the mouse's tail…they not what they say they are…talk big…but action not line up with words…vedy, vedy eye opening, but Jimmie not disappointed."

"No problem, I depend on Lord, not people.

Jimmy is richly blessed…deeply loved…highly favored." That belief guides him and determines his attitude and actions.

It's the Jimmys of this world who keep problems and disappointments in perspective. Their contagiousness and authenticity quickens the most church-hardened Christian. I saw Jimmy dine with some of the most sophisticated government officials and businessmen in Singapore, yet serve the most poor and needy in the elderly housing flats. He is loved and respected by both groups. He doesn't see distinctions in people, he sees Jesus in people!

....

That's authentic Christianity—giving the church back to the community through the belief that Christians are "richly blessed, deeply loved, and highly favored."

6

Experts and Learners

One of my challenges as a public speaker is that people think I'm an expert. While I do have *something* to say in my area of expertise, I don't have *everything* to say. It is easy for me, as well as other "experts," to begin to believe their own press. Many experts have more degrees than a thermometer, but that doesn't make them expert in *everything*, just an expert in *their thing*. In fact, many experts become "ex-spurts"!

The following story came from an e-mail I received a few years ago.

Once upon a time a sheepherder was tending his sheep at the edge of a country road in rural Wyoming. A brand new Jeep Grand Cherokee screeched to a halt next to him. The driver, a young man dressed in a very expensive suit and tie, designer shoes, Gucci sunglasses, a Rolex wristwatch, jumped out and asked the herder, "If I guess how many sheep you have, will you give me one of them?" The herder looked at the young man, then looked at the sprawling heard of grazing sheep and said, "OK."

The young man parked his vehicle, connected his notebook and wireless modem, entered a NASA site, scanned the ground using satellite imagery and a GPS, opened a database and 60 Excel tables filled with algorithms, then printed a 150-page report on his high-tech mini printer. He turned to the herder and said, "You have exactly 1,586 sheep here." The herder answered, "Say, you're right. Pick out a sheep." The young man took one of the animals and put it in the back of his Jeep.

As he was preparing to drive away, the herder looked at him and asked, "Now, if I guess your profession, will you pay me back in kind?"

"Sure!" the young man answered.

"You're a consultant."

"Exactly! How did you know?" asked the young man.

"Very simple. First you came here without being invited. Second, you charged me a fee to tell me something I already knew. Third, you do not understand anything about my business, and I'd really like to have my dog back."

Proverbs 1:5 says, "A wise man will hear and increase in learning, and a man of understanding will acquire wise counsel." In other words,

in areas where we are not an expert, we need to become learners.

That's hard for us experts, isn't it? In regard to spiritual things, read the Bible and attend a Bible-believing church. And go with a mind to learn from The Expert—God. After all, your mind is like a parachute, it works best when it's open!

· ·

Finding God by learning about Him in the Bible is the surest way to discover His unfailing love for you.

7

Enjoy Your Coffee

I am a coffee lover. The stronger the better, especially in the morning. Recently, I was in downtown Seattle standing in front of the original Starbucks at Pike Place Farmer's Market. Now that's good duty! Being a coffee lover I couldn't help but notice this story that came through the Internet.

A group of alumni, highly established in their careers, got together to visit one of their university professors. The conversation soon turned into complaints about stress in work and life. After offering his guests refreshments, the professor went to the kitchen and returned with a large pot of coffee and an assortment of cups. Some were porcelain, others were plastic, glass, and crystal. Some were plain, others were expensive and quite exquisite. He told his guests to help themselves to the coffee.

When all the students had a cup of coffee in hand, he said, "If you noticed, all the nice-looking, expensive cups were chosen first, leaving the plain and cheap ones. While it is normal for you to want only the best for yourselves, that is the source of your problems and stress. Be assured that the cup itself adds no quality to the coffee. In most cases, the name-brand and exquisite cups just make things more expensive and, in some cases, even hide what we drink. What all of you really wanted was coffee, not the cup. Yet, you all consciously went for the best cups. Then you even began eyeing each other's cups.

"Now consider this. Life is the coffee—jobs, money, and position in society are the cups. They are just tools to hold and contain life. The type of cup we have does not define or change the quality of life we live. Sometimes, by concentrating only on the cup, we fail to enjoy the coffee God has provided for us."[14]

That's a good lesson for us all. We have all played the comparison game. We have to have a better cup than someone else. We try to outdo others and become undone in the process. Sometimes when you try to possess the best cups, the best cups end up possessing you. Why not just enjoy who we are, who they are, and enjoy the coffee of life.

Sometimes people are like cups, they don't look or act like the fancy cups you prefer, but if you enjoy the coffee in the cup, life gets better!

It's what is inside the cup that counts to God.

God brews the coffee, not the cups. So, enjoy your coffee—you're a special blend!

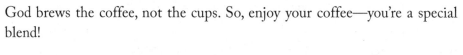

Peace starts with a smile—and a good cup of coffee. Make mine strong and dark. I'll be glad to take it in a paper cup!

8

It Could Be Worse!

With all the disasters going on in the world, it can be a challenge to think positively about the future.

A father, passing by his son's bedroom, was astonished to see the bed was nicely made and everything was picked up and put in its place. Then he saw an envelope propped up on the pillow. It was addressed to Dad. Fearing the worst, he opened the envelope and read the letter with trembling hands.

Dear Dad,

It is with great regret and sorrow that I'm writing you. I had to elope with my new girlfriend because I wanted to avoid a scene with Mom and you. I've been finding real passion with Stacy. She is so nice. But I know you would not approve of her because of all her piercings, tattoos, tight motorcycle clothes, and because she is so much older than me. But it's not only the passion. Dad, she's pregnant. She says we will be very happy. She owns a trailer in the woods and has a stack of firewood for the whole winter.

We share a dream of having more children. Stacy has opened my eyes to the fact that marijuana doesn't really hurt anyone. We will be growing it for ourselves as well as trading it with all the other people in the commune for all the cocaine and ecstasy we want. In the meantime, we will pray that science finds a cure for AIDS so Stacy can get better. She sure deserves it.

Don't worry, Dad. I'm 15 and know how to take care of myself. Someday I'm sure I will be back to visit so you can get to know your grandchildren.

Love,

Your son, John

P.S. Dad, none of the above is true. I'm over at Tommy's house. I just wanted to remind you that there are worse things in life than the report card that's in my center desk drawer. I love you! Call me when it is safe for me to come home.[15]

Yes, things could be worse.

An optimist thinks that this is the best possible world. A pessimist fears that this is true.

Most things are not as bad as they first appear to be. The Bible has much to say about times like these. The Bible gives us wisdom to get through crisis times. If we are smart enough to read it and ask God to reveal His plan for us, things will get better—not worse!

My suggestion in times like these, read John 14:1-3. Look up Philippians 4:6-9. How about Romans 8:26-39, or Matthew 6:25-34? Psalm 23 is always wonderful. Dust off that Bible of yours. Read it and get God's opinion on the situation. Let the Holy Spirit speak to you. Don't let your worries get the best of you. After all, Moses started out as a basket case, and ended up leading a nation!

•••

Make sure that your character is free from the love of money, being content with what you have; for He Himself has said, "I will never desert you, nor will I ever forsake you" (Hebrews 13:5).

9

Remembering What
Not To Forget

It's summer in America and the major league baseball season is in full swing. Not so in high school baseball though. The season is over, much to my son Jon's disappointment. Jon just finished his Junior year in high school, and next year he will be at the top of the food chain. It took him 12 years to do that and none too soon, in his opinion.

Jon was the starting left fielder on his high school baseball team. He had a tremendous year. He raised his batting average almost 300 percent over the previous year. He made some fantastic catches. He also had a three wins to one loss record as a pitcher with some complete games. He was voted honorable mention in his division. But what he was most excited about, as was his coach and team, was his hitting.

Then Jon got into a hitting slump during the state finals. Try as he might, he just couldn't find the ball. It wasn't for lack of effort. He was probably 50 percent of the May sales of the local batting cages. He would practice after his team practiced.

The slump affected his fielding too. Jon missed a few fly balls that would have been normal, uneventful catches in the regular season. He was worried that he would be benched in the most important games of the year. He even got to the point when he wanted to be taken out of the game. But his coach stuck with him, even in the playoffs. The coach remembered how Jon played in the regular season.

It's nice when people remember you, isn't it?

It's nice when people remember how you have affected or contributed to their life in the past. However, people tend to forget, don't they? The "what have you done for me lately, live in the present" mentality dictates minds today. Especially in the playoffs of life. You have to perform or you're out. Jon would agree that he should have been replaced. But the coach got a return on his investment next year from Jon. Why? Someone very important in his life remembered him during the hard times.

God doesn't forget your works for Him, your love toward Him, and your concern for people. Even those works you have done in the past—God doesn't forget! That's the lesson Jon learned from the coach.

....

For God is not unjust so as to forget your work and the love which you have shown toward His name, in having ministered and in still ministering to the saints (Hebrews 6:10).

10

Lessons From a Parrot

Dick received a parrot for his birthday. This parrot was fully grown, with a bad attitude, and even worse vocabulary. Every other word the parrot spoke was an expletive. Those that weren't expletives were, to say the least, rude.

Dick tried hard to change the bird's attitude and was constantly saying polite words, playing soft music, and doing everything he could think of to try and set a good example. But nothing worked. He yelled at the bird and the bird got worse. He shook the bird and the bird got more angry and more rude. Finally, in a moment of desperation, Dick put the parrot in the freezer.

For a few moments, Dick heard the bird squawking and kicking and screaming. Then, suddenly there was quiet. Dick was frightened that he might have actually hurt the bird, so he quickly opened the freezer door. The parrot calmly stepped out onto Dick's extended arm and said: "I am sorry that I might have offended you with my language and actions, and ask for your forgiveness. I will endeavor to correct my behavior."

Dick was astounded at the bird's change of attitude. He was just about to ask the parrot what had made such a drastic change in his attitude, when the parrot spoke again and said: "May I ask what the chicken did?"

The parrot needed something drastic to happen to change his attitude. Sometimes we need something drastic to happen that makes us stop and think. These encounters can change us—hopefully for the better. Encounters like the one the parrot had cause us to wake up, shake up, and put on our makeup. They open the eyes of our hearts, and give us a glimpse of where we are as compared to where we could be. Drastic encounters flush the quail out of the bushes of our lives. These experiences are red lights on the dashboards of our lives signaling us to change, do something different, make an adjustment—if we don't, we will encounter danger and expensive repairs ahead.

Remember, your talent is God's gift to you. However, what you do with your talent is your gift to God. God wants to prepare you for what He has ready for you. Being prepared is also your responsibility. Good attitude and character are what move you from unfulfilled potential to fulfilled reality.

You can't change your character by getting a facelift. Character and attitude is an inside job.

Take the first step toward changing your situation. It is my sincere desire for you to reach your dream, vision, goal, and destiny. It's God's desire too! So when those drastic, attention-getting times come, it may be God getting you ready for what He has for you. Learn from the parrot—adjust the attitude and go for gratitude. God wants to give us more than just crackers!

....

"For I know the plans I have for you" declares the Lord, *"plans to prosper you and not to harm you, plans to give you hope and a future"* (Jeremiah 29:11).

11

Two or Three to Agree

A man was lost while driving through the country. As he tried to read a road map, he accidentally drove off the road into a ditch. Though he wasn't injured, his car was stuck deep in mud. So the man walked to a nearby farm to ask for help.

"Warwick can get you out of that ditch," said the farmer, pointing to an old mule standing in the field. The man looked at the haggardly old mule and looked at the farmer who repeated, "Yep, Warwick can do the job." The man figured he had nothing to lose, so the two men and Warwick made their way back to the ditch.

The farmer hitched the mule to the car. With the snap of the reins he shouted, "Pull, Fred! Pull, Jack! Pull, Ted! Pull, Warwick!" And the mule pulled the car from the ditch with very little effort.

The man was amazed. He thanked the farmer, patted the mule and asked, "Why did you call out all of those other names before you called Warwick?"

The farmer grinned and said, "Old Warwick is just about blind. As long as he believes he is part of a team, he doesn't mind pulling."[16]

The first thing Jesus did when He started His ministry was form a team. He knew the power and sustainability of teamwork. He knew that none of us are as smart as all of us. He knew that one cannot multiply. He knew that in order to make a melody, partners must first play in harmony. We grow more by a positive partnership than by trying to go it alone.

President Woodrow Wilson said, "We should not only use all the brains we have, but all the brains we can borrow."[17] Behind every able man there are always other able men and women. Someone once said partnership is the ability to work together toward a common vision—the ability to direct individual accomplishment toward organized objectives. Working together is the fuel that allows common people to attain uncommon results. Simply put, it is less "me" and more "we." Benjamin Franklin, at the signing of the Declaration of Independence, said it perfectly, "We must all hang together, else we shall all hang together"[18] Hear that politicians?

Sometimes partnerships may feel the least comfortable when the most necessary. Right now, with all the tensions in our nation and world, it is wise to check out what the Bible says about teamwork. God models it in the Trinity. The prophet Amos says, "Can two people walk together without agreeing to meet?" God put 12 tribes together and made them one nation. Psalm 133 says that where "brothers dwell together in unity...there the Lord commands the blessing." See that? Most of those teamwork guru's get their material from the Bible!

Mark Twain wrote,

"It is amazing what can be done if no one minds who gets the credit."[19]

Just ask Warwick!

••

For where two or three have gathered together in My name, I am there in their midst (Matthew 18:20).

12

Have You Ever Seen God?

A kindergarten teacher was observing her classroom of children while they were drawing. She would occasionally walk around to see each child's work. She asked one little girl, who was working very diligently, about her drawing. The girl replied, "I'm drawing God." The teacher paused and said, "But nobody knows what God looks like." Without missing a beat or looking up from her drawing, the little girl replied, "They will when I'm finished!"

Now there's confidence for you! I'd like to see that picture, how about you? In fact, children hold a very special place in the eyes of God. Jesus was a child advocate. When grownups tried to stop children from approaching Jesus, He stated rather emphatically, "Permit the children to come to Me, and stop hindering them, for the kingdom of God belongs to such as these" (Luke 18:16).

Perhaps that girl was seeing something we adults can't see quite as clearly. It is true that to see God, one has to approach God not as an expert, but as a learner. We adults like to form God into our own image. We define God rather than letting God define Himself. Sometimes God defines Himself by what He does, such as in Psalm chapter 23 when He is David's good Shepherd. Let's look at David's image of God after many years of getting to know God firsthand. God paints His picture of what He looks like through David, just like that little girl knew who she was drawing.

The Lord is my Shepard—*that's relationship*. I shall not want—*that's supply*. He makes me to lie down in green pastures—*that's rest*. He leads me beside still waters—*that's refreshment*. He restores my soul—*that's healing*. He leads me in paths of righteousness—*that's guidance*. For His name's sake—*that's purpose*. Yea, though I walk through the valley of the shadow of death—*that's testing*. I will fear no evil—*that's protection*.

For Thou are with me—*that's faithfulness*. Thy rod and Thy staff they comfort me—*that's discipline*. Thou prepareth a table before me in the presence of my enemies—*that's hope*. Thou anointest my head with oil—*that's consecration*. My cup runs over—*that's abundance*. Surely goodness and mercy shall follow me all the days of my life—*that's blessing*. And I will dwell in the house of the Lord—*that's security*. Forever—*that's eternity*. That's certainly a very credible image, I would say!

For many years I had the wrong definition of God. It hurt me much more than helped me. I was mistaken about God. I thought I was an expert, instead of the learner I needed to be. Hint!

Learn from others' mistakes, the second mouse gets the cheese!

....

God:
Is your best friend.
Supplies your every need.
Provides rest and refreshment.
Heals every wound.
Guides you to your purpose
Tests and protects.
Is faithful.
Disciplines in love.
Gives you hope.
Provides consecrates through Jesus Christ.
Desires for you abundant blessings.
Is your security throughout eternity.

13

A Lesson From a Donkey

These are amazing days when we see gifted leaders, politicians, ministers, and CEOs keep making the same mistakes over and over again. In the quest for being number one in profitability, adulation, or control, more times than not, these well-meaning leaders become victims of their own conquests. It doesn't matter which political party, theology, company, or industry, the same problem keeps occurring. The results are devastating, to those directly involved, as well as their families, and society.

What is the problem? In most cases, pride. Pride puffs us up and can quickly knock us down. It's hard to have success, sustainability, and stability when the foundation is based on pride. Having a solid base founded on biblical principles will build a great legacy in all areas of life.

I want to make sure that we avoid the pitfalls of leaders like King Nebuchadnezzar in Babylon. Look what Daniel says in the Bible about this king. "The supreme God made Nebuchadnezzar a great king and gave him dignity and majesty...but he became proud, stubborn, and cruel, and he was removed from his royal throne and lost his place of honor." (See Daniel 5:20.) Wow—how many of us have been there, seen that, maybe even done that, *and* got the T-shirt?!

Jesus knew the dangers of pride. That's why He hung around donkeys, not horses. Common sense and tradition says He was carried to Bethlehem in the womb of His mother who was riding on a donkey. When He arrived in Jerusalem one week before His crucifixion, He was riding a donkey. The

Bible uses the words, "gentle, and mounted on a donkey…the foal of a beast of burden." (See Matthew 21:5.)

As Jesus came into Jerusalem, people were waving palm branches and carrying on. Can you imagine the donkey carrying Jesus? Perhaps the donkey thought, *They are cheering for me! I'm such a great donkey! I'm the one! Who's your daddy? I'm anointed, appointed, elected, perfected, selected, and connected! I'm blessed…get me on television…hee-haw!*

Donkeys like this become the word that the King James version of the Bible uses for donkeys. Enough said!

The donkey *carried* Jesus, but was *not* Jesus. Jesus chose the donkey, the donkey didn't choose Him.

The donkey was chosen to *carry* a message, not to *be* the message.

Many politicians, CEOs, gifted leaders, and ministers would have a more positive and endearing legacy if they could learn the lesson of the gentle, humble donkey. We are carrying the vision, we are not the vision! We are the servant, not what is being served! Don't take the glory; *give* the glory to whom it belongs—God.

Here are some hints to keep pride and self-importance at bay. Always keep your words soft and sweet, just in case you have to eat them. Always read materials that will make you look good if you die while reading. Drive carefully—not just cars are recalled by their maker. It may be your sole purpose in life is simply to serve as a warning to others. The only difference between run and ruin is 'i.'

· ·

Donkey talk:
Keep your words soft and sweet.
Read good stuff.
Maneuver carefully through life.
Run from ruin.

14

Your Health and Prosperity

Joseph Richardson, a New York millionaire, lived and died in a house only 5 feet wide. It was called the "Spite House," and it deserved its name. Owning the narrow lot of land on which it was built, Mr. Richardson wished to sell it to the neighboring property owners. They would not pay him what he asked. In spite, he built a 5-foot-wide disfigured house which hurt the property values of everyone on the block—and then he condemned himself to an uncomfortable life of living in it.[20]

Greg Anderson said that everything is created twice, first mentally, then physically.[21] The Bible speaks of this idea in a most amazing verse, "Beloved, I pray that in all respects you may prosper and be in good health, just as your soul prospers" (3 John 2).

You will prosper and be in good health as your soul, which is your mind, will, and emotions prosper. That means that your thinker, chooser, and feeler are under the control of wisdom, discernment, and discretion. You work best when you are wisdom-driven, not emotion-driven. You will have a more positive attitude about yourself, others, and life in general when your soul is prospering. This truth could have really helped the man who built the Spite House.

Many folks these days are struggling with soul prosperity. Consequently, their physical health is often the victim of this struggle. They are like the man who went to the psychiatrist with a severe identity crisis, saying, "Doctor, I'm convinced I'm a dog." When the psychiatrist asked how long he had this problem, he blurted out, "Ever since I was a puppy!" It's easy to lose our soul health, isn't it?

One of the major causes of soul sickness is what author and speaker Zig Ziglar calls *attitudosis*. He says attitudosis is a condition brought on by your neglect of others and their needs, and your extreme focus on and excessive attention to the minuscule aches, pains, and inconveniences in your live.[22] He is not talking about real crisis but oversensitivity to small things like the millionaire living in the 5-foot-wide house.

Honesty is a thing I have no problem with until I get honest about it. Humility is being honestly and sincerely willing to learn from other people, having no desire to strangle them in the process. Sometimes taking a good, truthful look at ourselves can spring us into action and a more freeing perspective of life and our problems. Whatever we can tolerate, we can't change. When Dallas Cowboys' coach Tom Landry was asked what it takes to build a winning football team he said,

"My job is to get men to do what they don't want to do in order to achieve what they've always wanted to achieve."

Live long and prosper!

....

Love is when listening to you is more fun than thinking about me. Persecuted is the way I feel when I get what I deserve. Powerless is a human being without faith in God.

15

Pieces or Peace?

Two men were shipwrecked on an island. One started screaming and yelling. "We're going to die, we're going to die! There's no food, no water! We're going to die!" The second man was leaning up against a palm tree so calmly that it drove the first man crazy. "Don't you understand? We're going to die!"

The second man replied, "You just don't understand. I make 100,000 dollars a week."

The first man looked at him quite dumbfounded and asked, "What difference does that make? We're on an island with no food and no water. We're going to die...we're going to die!"

The second man answered, "You just don't get it. I make 100,000 dollars a week and I give 10 percent of that to my church every week. My pastor will find me!"[23]

Now that's what I call peace!

You might be saying, "But I don't make 100,000 a week." I hear you...me neither! But I've been on that island, haven't you? Yet, here we are, we made it somehow. I have found that through the good times and the not-so-good times, God was always with me. You might think that it was coincidence that finally got you out of the mess. However, could it be that coincidence is when God chooses to remain anonymous?

You might be thinking, "Problems, problems, why do I have so many problems?" Did you ever think that problems and tough times can bring you closer to God and resources you would have never discovered any other way?

Here are a few quotes from some great leaders that might help you with your problems:

Some minds and perspectives are like concrete, thoroughly mixed up and permanently set. Problems can break up our self-sufficiency like a sledge hammer can break up concrete. In the midst of the thorns, you discover the rose.

There's a secret to getting through those shipwrecked-on-an-island times. There's a way to go from pieces to peace. Here it is. Mastered by God, you can control how you react to circumstances, people, and calamity. Mastered by anything less than God, you are a victim or puppet of circumstances, people, or calamity. I like to say during tough times: I will, by my life's choices, prove that the Word of God is true.

That brings God into the picture. It takes resolve and humility to do that. When you're against something big, face it head on with God by your side.

"He was easier than the lion and the bear. In fact, he was so big I couldn't miss him!" That was David writing about Goliath.

You see, you can go to pieces or have peace. God is a lifesaver. The Bible says that God is a very present help in times of trouble—and you don't have to make $100,000 a week to secure His services!

•••

Peace I leave with you; My peace I give to you; not as the world gives do I give to you Do not let your heart be troubled, nor let it be fearful (John 14:27).

16

Beginergy

A local news station was interviewing an 80-year-old woman who was married—for the fourth time. The interviewer asked her questions about her life, about what it felt like to be marrying again at 80, and then about her new husband's occupation.

"He's a funeral director," she said.

"Interesting," the newsman said. Then he asked her if she wouldn't mind telling him a little about her first three husbands and what they did for a living. She paused to reflect upon those years, then a smile came to her face. She said that she had first married a banker when she was in her early 20s, then a circus ringmaster when in her 40s, later a preacher when in her 60s, and now in her 80s a funeral director.

The interviewer looked at her quite astonished and asked why she had married four men with such diverse careers.

"I married one for the money, two for the show, three to get ready, and four to go." Ha!

Whether she had major relationship skill issues or was the recipient of others' choices or circumstances, she certainly didn't have a very good batting average in the area of marriage. However, she does have "beginergy." Beginergy is the energy and resiliency to start over again. It is the ability to get past the past, close the chapter and begin again. Actually it's more than finishing a chapter, it's putting down one book and starting another. If you are a Jane Austin fan, it's finishing Pride and Prejudice and beginning Sense and Sensibility.

Too many people are entangled in the past. Their minds are like over-loaded computers full of viruses that keep slowing down their thoughts. They live on the stale bread of the past rather than enjoying the fresh bread of the future.

God know that we can easily get stuck in the woulda, coulda, shoulda's of life. But He gives us Good News! Remember Peter after denying Christ three times? Or the woman caught in adultery? Or the woman at the well who had five husbands? Or the tax-gatherer? They all received another chance, a new start, a new attitude, a new outlook. They were healed, accepted, even forgiven when they took responsibility and asked for forgive-ness. God gave them beginergy. God emptied them to fill them.

That's what is so amazing about grace.

The Scripture says in Psalm 32:1 in The Message, "Count yourselves lucky, how happy you must be—you get a new start, your slate is wiped clean." That's what I call a spiritual mulligan! My advice is to be sure you have the beginergy to get ready before we go.

....

...and four to go!

17

To Tell the Truth

A fisherman from the city was out fishing on a lake in a small boat. He noticed another man in a small boat open his tackle box and take out a mirror. Being curious, the man rowed over and asked, "What is the mirror for?"

"That's my secret way to catch fish," said the other man. "Shine the mirror on the top of the water. The fish notice the spot of sun on the water above and they swim to the surface. Then I just reach down, net them, and pull them into the boat."

"Wow! Does that really work?"

"You bet it does."

"Would you be interested in selling that mirror? I'll give you $30 for it."

"Well, OK."

After the money was transferred, the city fisherman asked, "By the way, how many fish have you caught this week?"

"You're the sixth," he said.[24]

Have you noticed that today's world is a world of partial truths and opinions that we call truth? It seems like everyone puts their own spin on truth. As a result, we have more and more fishermen selling their mirrors to the gullible "catch a fish at any cost" crowd. Life-guiding philosophies and opinions that are being formed by agenda-driven sound bites may very well be the Trojan horse in our society these days.

Very few have the time or desire to investigate if what is being said is truth or someone's own agenda-twisted truth.

The truth is, the *whole truth* will set you free. It's worth taking the time to check out what is true, honorable, right, and excellent. Don't entrust your life to those who play on your emotions to advance their agendas. Your life is too important for that.

The Bereans knew the danger of that fisherman with mirrors. The Bible says that the Bereans were more noble-minded than those in Thessalonica, for they received the word with great eagerness, examining the Scriptures daily, to see whether these things were so (see Acts 17:11).

Whether what is being said consists of half truths or truth just being derailed by our or another's mental roadblocks, we need to be aware of those fishermen with mirrors. Our country, our life, and our future may depend on it.

Consider these principles: *Discretion* is recognizing and avoiding words, actions, and attitudes that could bring undesirable attitudes. *Wisdom* is seeing and responding to life's situations from a perspective that transcends current circumstances. *Virtue* is the moral excellence evident in life to consistently do what is right...not just expedient.

Truthfulness is earning future trust by accurately reporting past facts. *Sincerity* is the eagerness to do what is right with transparent motives. *Persuasiveness* is guiding vital truths around another's mental roadblocks. Finally, *alertness* is being aware of our surroundings so we can respond rightly.[25]

•••

Jesus said to him, "I am the way, and the truth, and the life; no one comes to the Father but through Me" (John 14:6).

18

The Way We Are

A priest was walking along the school corridor near the preschool wing when a group of little ones were trotting by on the way to the cafeteria. One little boy of three or four stopped and looked at him in his clerical clothes and asked, "Why do you dress funny?"

He told the little boy that he was a priest and that is the uniform that priests wear.

Then the boy pointed to the priest's plastic collar insert and asked, "Does it hurt? Do you have a boo-boo?"

The priest was perplexed until he realized that to the boy the collar looked like a Band-Aid. So the priest took it off to show the boy. The little guy noticed the words on the collar that cited the name of the manufacturer. The priest asked, "Do you know what those words say?"

"Yes, I do," said the lad who was not old enough to read. Peering intently at the letters, he said, "Kills ticks and fleas up to six months!"[26]

Now, there is quite a lesson here. We humans tend to see things the way *we* are as opposed to the way *they* are. The all or nothing world of politics is an example. It's a world where opinions are called truth. Each side tends to make everything into its own image. One side can see an issue as an inconvenient truth while the other side sees the same issue as a convenient lie. Someone once said that politics is the art of making your selfish desires seem like the national interest. But the same could be said about church, business, education, or media. Wherever you have people, you will have opinions.

Where's the truth? Usually somewhere in the middle. Opinion rules and discernment drools. The result? Less and less truth and more and more polarization. Don't get me wrong. Opinions are crucial, but wouldn't it be a good idea to make an intelligent decision rather than an emotional decision? Learn to discern. That way you have real fact backing you up, not someone else's talking point or sound bite.

The Bible says in Proverbs 20:25, "It is a trap for a man to say rashly, 'It is holy!' and after the vows to make inquiry." In other words, when you rashly and quickly get moved by the moment or medium, form an opinion, and not research it, it can come back to haunt you.

The Bible says wisdom is shouting in the streets, "Can you here me?" Wisdom, in my opinion, is what is needed in these outraged times we live in. Wisdom says, "be quick to hear, slow to speak, and slow to anger." Wisdom doesn't demonize or marginalize unless backed up with facts. Wisdom offers real and tangible solutions, not finger pointing. Wisdom looks for a way in, not a way out.

Wisdom is based on facts, not emotions.

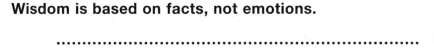

Offer informed answers to real issues; otherwise, we offer,
"Kills fleas and ticks for up to six months."

19

Axes and Lumberjacks

Did you hear about the two lumberjacks who challenged each other to see which one could cut down more trees in a day? At daybreak, the first one began furiously chopping down trees. He worked up a sweat and by noon he had cut down 16 trees. Meanwhile the other lumberjack had only cut down four trees, because he took the first two hours to sharpen his axe.

As he sharpened the axe, his challenger laughed at him, thinking he was doomed to lose the bet because of all the wasted time. That's when things got interesting. By early afternoon, the first lumberjack was slowing down. It took him almost an hour to cut down one tree, while his friend was picking up speed.

How could this be? Certainly he was as strong as his friend. Strength had little to do with it. It was all about whose axe was sharper. The sharper the axe, the quicker the trees came down. By late afternoon the second lumberjack who had sharpened his axe had passed his friend by several trees and won easily.[27]

The Scriptures say in Ecclesiastes 10:10, "If the axe is dull and he does not sharpen its edge, then he must exert more strength. Wisdom has the advantage of giving success." God gives us great advice here. That first lumberjack would have greatly increased his probability of success if he would have used some wisdom and sharpened his axe...before the contest. Wisdom increases your chance of success. Working hard without wisdom seldom wins out over working smart with wisdom.

Wisdom doesn't always come with age; sometimes age comes alone!

Let's look at a few quotes[28] from wise people who can sharpen your axe for success. Arthur Howard says, "If you stop learning today, you stop leading tomorrow." Another quote is from Disraeli, "As a rule, he or she who has the most information will have the greatest success in life." The first lumberjack had surely run into this before but never learned the lesson. Thomas Edison said, "Everything comes to those who hustle while they wait." That second lumberjack knew that. He invested in down time in order to make up time!

Charles Burton said, "You will never find time for anything. If you want time, you must make it." Effective people do the important things first. Effective people know that urgent and vital are two different things. The first lumberjack did what was urgent. The second lumberjack did what was vital. See the difference? Bob Costas says, "Champions don't become champions in the field, they are merely recognized there." You see, first be best, then be first! That second lumberjack had the contest won before he won the contest. Why? He had the wisdom to be sharp and stay sharp.

....

Don't just bludgeon your way though life, get some axe-sharpening wisdom from the Scriptures and wise people with character. It will help you to be successful both spiritually and naturally!

20

Stuck in the Middle With You!

When we moved cross-country, my wife and I decided to drive both of our cars. Nathan, our 8-year-old, worriedly asked, "How will we keep from getting separated?"

"We'll drive slowly so that one car can follow the other," I reassured him.

"Yeah, but what if we do get separated?" he persisted.

"Well, then I guess we'll never see each other again," I quipped.

"OK," he said. "I'm riding with Mom!"

As I write, my wife and I are nearing the end of a Caribbean Cruise. Our cruise ship has a glass elevator, and one of the couples traveling with us was happily on their way to the 12th floor when the elevator stopped—right between the 10th and 11th floors. It wouldn't move.

They tried the emergency phone. No answer. Then they tried the emergency alarm. No sound, no response, no nothing. Because this happened after midnight, most people were in their cabins. Fortunately our party of eight had four walkie talkies between us. All of a sudden, we get the "Houston, we've got a problem" call. "Help, we need somebody…help, not just anybody…help!"

Soon there was a whole gallery of people looking at the stranded couple from both the right side and the left side of the 10th and 11th floors. The couple recalled that they now know what fish in a fish bowl feel like. They became the late-night entertainment, which made me think of the song lyrics, "Clowns to the right of me, jokers to the left, here I am, stuck in the middle with you."

For the next hour or so, we all had great fun at the couple's expense. Finally, help arrived and everything turned out fine. When the couple finally arrived at the 12th floor lounge, they were greeted with a standing ovation. The "elevator couple" incident became well-known shipwide.

The point of this true story?

When you are handed a situation you don't like or didn't anticipate, it sure is nice to have friends you can share it with.

The Bible says, "There is a friend who sticks closer than a brother." Believe me, you just may want one of those walkie talkie friends or elevator advocates the next time you get stuck in the middle of a situation where nobody knows you. Oh by the way, God's walkie talkie is always tuned in to your frequency.

•••

What's better than "riding with mom"? Knowing that God is beside you every step along your life's journey.

21

Is Your Hut on Fire?

Everyone goes through problems once and awhile. We often say, "Why do problems always happen to *me*? Isn't it somebody *else's* turn?" We all think like that from time to time, don't we? I found in the 25 years I've been ministering that there are always people somewhere who need hope. They need someone to lift their countenance. Someone to say that the light at the end of the tunnel is not a train coming straight at them! If you need to know that, read on.

There is a story circulating on the Internet titled, "Is Your Hut on Fire?" It reads as follows. The only survivor of a shipwreck was washed up on a small, uninhabited island. He prayed feverishly for God to rescue him, but no help seemed forthcoming.

Exhausted, he eventually managed to build a little hut out of driftwood to protect himself from the elements and to store a few possessions. One day after scavenging for food, he arrived home to find his little hut in flames, the smoke rolling into the sky. The worst had happened and everything was lost. He was stunned with grief and anger. He cried out, "God, how could you do this to me?"

Early the next day, he was awakened by the sound of an approaching ship coming to rescue him. "How did you know I was here?" asked the weary man of his rescuers. "We saw your smoke signal!" they replied.

Many times when we are down to nothing, God is up to something. When you are at your wit's end, you will find God lives there. The will of

God will never take you to where the grace of God will not protect you. It is easy to get discouraged when things are going bad. Don't lose heart, God is at work in your life, even in the midst of tough stuff! Don't tell God how big the mountain is, tell the mountain how big God is. Don't magnify your problem, magnify the Lord.

Peace in the storm starts with perspective, doesn't it? Remember, every miracle starts with a problem!

Problems are the building blocks of miracles.

You can't have a miracle without a problem. God loves to calm the storms of our lives. It's a wonderful opportunity for Him to get the glory He deserves, isn't it?

God wants us to *walk through* the valley of the shadow of death, not *camp in* the valley of the shadow of death (see Psalm 23). Remember, the next time your little hut is burning to the ground, it just may be a smoke signal that summons the grace of God!

••

**Don't tell God how big the mountain is,
tell the mountain how big God is.**

22

Never, Never, Never, Never Give Up!

Many of you will recognize the title of this chapter as a quote by Winston Churchill, prime minister of Great Britain during World War II. His attitude of never giving up helped bring the war to a successful conclusion.

Author Phil Baker says that, "Achieving in life is not just being in the right place at the right time, but also being in the wrong place at the wrong time and not giving up." Successful people who persevere respond differently from other people. They don't look for escape. They look for lessons. Their problems make them, not break them. Baker goes on to say that we can easily make the mistake of thinking that successful people just get out there and succeed. In reality, most just get out there and stay there through failure after failure. Most people check out too soon. After all, by perseverance the snail reached the ark.[29]

The following is a quote by the all-time perseverance king—Abraham Lincoln. "Success is going from failure to failure without loss of enthusiasm." When the crowd is small and isn't with you, that's when the real you comes out. That's when you define your life and your legacy.

This next quote is from Ted Engstrom in *The Pursuit of Excellence* and it captures the concept of persevering for the right things.

Cripple him and you have a Sir Walter Scott. Lock him in a prison cell, and you have a John Bunyan. Bury him in the snows of Valley Forge, and you have a George Washington. Raise him in abject poverty, and you have an Abraham Lincoln. Strike him down with infantile paralysis, and he becomes Franklin Roosevelt.

Burn him so severely that the doctors say he will never walk again, and you have a Glen Cunningham—who set the world's one-mile record in 1934. Deafen him, and you have a Beethoven. Have him or her born black in a society filled with racial discrimination, and you have a Booker T. Washington, a Marian Andersen and a George Washington Carver. Call him a slow learner and "retarded" and write him off as uneducable, and you have an Albert Einstein.

You see—never, never, never, never quit!

Perseverance is part of the character of God.

If you tap into perseverance, you are tapping into a dimension of God that is unfathomable.

God will never, never, never, never give up on you!

....

By perseverance the snail reached the ark.

23

Never Been Better or Never Been Worse?

Here's a story that I think will inspire you—it inspired me. The author is unknown but the characters may be very familiar. My advice: as much as possible, be on the *never been better* side of life.

John is the kind of guy you love to hate. He is always in a good mood and always has something positive to say. When someone asks him how he's doing, he replies, "If I were any better, I'd be twins!"

I asked him one day, "I don't get it! You can't be a positive person all of the time. How do you do it?"

"Well," he said, "each morning I wake up and say to myself, you have two choices today. You can choose to be in a good mood or you can choose to be in a bad mood. I choose to be in a good mood. Each time something bad happens, I can choose to be a victim or I can choose to learn from it. I choose to learn from it. Every time someone comes to me complaining, I can choose to accept their complaints, or I can point out the positive side of life. I choose the positive side of life."

"Yeah, right, it's not that easy" I protested.

"Yes, it is," he said. "Life is all about choices. When you cut away all the junk, every situation is a choice. You choose how you react to situations. The bottom line: it's your choice how you live your life."

Several years later, I heard that John was involved in a serious accident, falling some 60 feet from a communications tower. After hours of surgery and weeks of intensive care, he was released from the hospital. I saw him about six months after the accident. When I asked him how he was, he replied, "If I were any better, I'd be twins. Wanna see my scars?"

I declined to see his wounds, but I did ask him what had gone through his mind as the incident took place. "The first thing that went through my mind was the well-being of my soon-to-be born daughter," he replied. "Then, as I lay on the ground, I remembered that I had two choices: I could choose to live or I could choose to die. I chose to live."

As they wheeled me into the emergency room and I saw the doctors' expressions I got scared. In their eyes, I read 'he's a dead man.'"

"What did you do?" I asked.

"Well, a big burly nurse asked if I was allergic to anything and I said 'YES—GRAVITY!'"

"Over their laughter, I said, 'Operate on me as if I am alive, not dead.'"

He lived, thanks to the skill of his doctors, but also because of his amazing attitude.

....

Therefore do not worry about tomorrow, for tomorrow will worry about itself. Each day has enough trouble of its own (Matthew 6:34 NKJV).

24

Gripe Sheets and Holding Patterns

I took a flight from Auckland to Wellington, New Zealand. My host had purchased a flight for me on Qantas Airlines, the national airline of Australia. Let me share with you something about Qantas Airlines and Australian culture that you will enjoy.

After every flight, Qantas pilots fill out a form called a gripe sheet that tells mechanics about problems with the aircraft. The mechanics correct the problems, document the repairs on the form, and then the pilots review the gripe sheets before the next flight.

Here are some actual maintenance complaints submitted by Qantas pilots and the solutions recorded by the maintenance engineers.[30] By the way, Qantas is the only major airline that has never had a major accident. Never let it be said that ground crews lack a sense of humor.

Pilot: Left inside main tire almost needs replacement.
Maintenance: Almost replaced left inside main tire.

Pilot: Test flight OK, except auto-land very rough.
Maintenance: Auto-land not installed on this aircraft.

Pilot: Something loose in cockpit.
Maintenance: Something tightened in cockpit.

Pilot: Dead bugs on windshield.
Maintenance: Live bugs on backorder.

Pilot: Evidence of leak on right main landing gear.
Maintenance: Evidence removed.

Pilot: DME volume unbelievably loud.
Maintenance: DME volume set to a more believable level.

Pilot: Suspected crack on windshield.
Maintenance: Suspect you're right.

Pilot: Number 3 engine missing.
Maintenance: Engine found on right wing after brief search.

Pilot: Aircraft handles funny.
Maintenance: Aircraft warned to straighten up, fly right, and be serious.

Pilot: Target radar hums.
Maintenance: Reprogrammed target radar with lyrics.

Pilot: Mouse in cockpit.
Maintenance: Cat installed.

Pilot: Noise coming from under instrument panel sounds like a midget
pounding on something with a hammer.
Maintenance: Took hammer away from midget.

If you're a seasoned air traveler, chances are you have had lots of gripes
about airlines and flying, but there are lots of lessons in life that you can learn
from the inconveniences of flying.

**Like flying, sometimes life puts us in holding patterns.
Holding patterns, though frustrating, are meant to allow tim-
ing and success to intersect.**

The primary objective is to have a successful, completed journey. The sec-
ondary objective is to be on time. Putting the second objective first can kill
you!

My favorite Bible verse is: "And it came to pass" (Gen. 8:6 KJV). When God puts you in a holding pattern, it's not just a question of having enough faith to receive His promises, it's also a matter of having enough spiritual staying power to stay airborne until it comes to pass. In your walk through life, it pays to have enough spiritual fuel and emotional intelligence to handle those delays and wait for clearance to land.

The Bible says "Wait for the Lord, be strong...let your heart take courage...." In other words, get a grip on those gripes.

....

And just like those Qantas pilots, don't be surprised if you receive some cheeky responses on your gripe sheets of life.

25

Gazing Forward

Have you ever seen a runner who ran a race backward and won? You know the answer. Yet many people are fixated on their past—past failures, past disappointments, even in a nostalgic way. Someone has said that the past is called the past because…it's past. That doesn't mean we should not learn from the past, but learning from and enjoying the past is not the same as being paralyzed by the past. Nostalgia is a wonderful servant but a terrible master.

In a sense, we should never build our future around the past. Author Mike Murdock points out this concept in the life of Jesus.

Jesus was born with a terrible stigma. His mother, Mary, was pregnant with Him before she ever married Joseph, her betrothed. The Bible says that they had not had a sexual relationship, but, "that which is conceived in her is of the Holy Spirit" (Matthew 1:20). Jesus never looked back. He never discussed the situation with anyone. There is not a single Scripture in the entire Bible where He ever brought up His background or His limitations.[31]

You see, there is no future to living in the past. Learn from it…yes! Enjoy it…yes! Get stuck in it…no!

My son, Jon, was on the Northwest Christian School varsity baseball team. The Bible verse for the year for the team was Proverbs 4:25, "Let your eyes look directly ahead, and let your gaze be fixed straight in front of you." That's great advice, especially for a bunch of young men who tend to forget all the good plays they make and gaze, or focus, on the mistakes they made. You don't play a baseball game facing backward!

The wonderful thing about gazing ahead is that it gives you a second chance. It gives you a new start. It transports one from the paralysis of analysis to productive forward motion.

Gazing ahead moves us from *the if only of yesterday and what if of tomorrow* to the *what is of today*.

God wants us to get our direction from Him, not the past! Stuff happens in life. Accept that some days you're the pigeon, and some days you're the statue. Even if you are on the right track, you'll get run over if you just sit there.

A truly happy person is one who can enjoy the scenery on a detour. After all, success is more by choice than it is by chance. Here's my advice. Close those chapters in your life that should have been closed a long time ago. You close those disabling chapters by forgiving yourself, or others, if necessary. Some people need to forgive God for their past or present circumstances. Playing victim is no fun and very costly—both to you and your community.

Nobody cares if you can't dance well, just get up and dance again. Get in the race and, for goodness sake, gaze forward. And just like Jesus, never mention or be limited by your past again. You can do it. I know it!

••

Accept that some days you're the pigeon,
and some days you're the statue.

26

Being Intimidated by Fear

Here's a fact that that I thought might interest you. According to author and pastor Warren Wiersbe, 92 percent of what we worry about never happens.[32] For instance:

A cowboy rode into town and stopped at the saloon for a drink. Unfortunately the locals had a habit of picking on strangers, of which he was one. When he finished his drink, he found that his horse had been stolen.

With surprising forcefulness he yelled, "Which one of you sidewinders stole my horse?" No one answered. "All right, I'm gonna have another drink and if my horse ain't back outside by the time I finish, I'm gonna do what I dun in Texas! And I don't like to have to do what I dun in Texas!"

Some of the locals shifted restlessly. The man, true to his word, had another drink, then he walked outside and his horse had been returned to the post. He saddled up and started to ride out of town.

The bartender wandered out of the bar and asked, "Say pardner, before you go I want to know what happened in Texas."

The cowboy turned back in his saddle, looked at the bartender, and said, "I had to walk home."

Now, there's an example of how to use intimidation and fear for your benefit. Lots of noise and intimidating words can play on your thinking process, can't it? Fear can move us from intelligent assessment to emotional distress quicker than you can say "Howdy pardner."

The cowboy created a picture of "what if" in the minds of the perpetrators. Fear took over because they didn't know who they were dealing with. To use Bible language, they had never been this way before! That's what the unknown can do to us, can't it? Fear can easily stop us in our tracks, make us lose our bearings, and cause us to underachieve.

I've been told that the Bible exhorts us to "fear not" 365 times in the Scriptures. That's one "fear not" for everyday of the year.

I don't think that is a coincidence, do you? "Fear not" is what we humans need. We need faith that everything is going to be OK. God has things under control. God may not be there when you think you need Him, but He is always right on time!

Don't let intimidation rule you. Unfounded or imaginary fear is like throwing logs on a fire. Faith in God is like water. Stop throwing logs on the fire and douse the fire with water. Faith does to fear what water does to fire.

The Bible says in Second Timothy that God has not given us a spirit of fear. That's good news! The world is rife with trials, hurts, speculations and false intimidations that are designed to play on our emotional well-being. However, don't embrace the kind of fear that incapacitates you for life.

••

Franklin D. Roosevelt (32nd President of the U.S.) said,
"The only thing we have to fear is fear itself."
That's good and godly advice for us today.

27

A Little Dog Philosophy

Believe it or not, Fido can provide some healthy spiritual insight for humans.

Someone once said, "The reason a dog has so many friends is because he wags his tail instead of his tongue." Ann Landers wrote, "Don't accept your dog's admiration as conclusive evidence that you are wonderful." Ben Williams reports, "There is no psychiatrist in the world like a puppy licking your face." "The average dog is a nicer person than the average person," says Andy Rooney.

Robert Benchley says, "A dog teaches a boy fidelity, perseverance, and to turn around three times before lying down." Rita Rudner quips, "I wonder if other dogs think poodles are members of a weird religious cult." "Anybody who doesn't know what soap tastes like has never washed a dog," says Franklin P. Jones. Someone said, "If your dog is fat, you aren't getting enough exercise." I like that one because my dog is skinny, but she is also 15 years old!

But wait, there's more! Joe Weinstein says, "My dog is worried about the economy because Alpo is up to $3.00 a can. That's almost $21.00 in dog money." Ann Taylor observes, "Ever consider what dogs think of us? I mean, here we come from a grocery store with the most amazing haul; chicken, pork, and half a cow. They must think we're the greatest hunters on earth."

"If you think dogs can't count, try putting three dog biscuits in your pocket and then give him only two of them," quips Phil Pastoret. "Women and cats will do as they please, men and dogs should relax and get used to the idea," observes Robert Heinlein.

Now, let me make an observation from dogs about man and his relationship to God. There are two Greek words for the word *worship* in the New Testament in the Bible. One word is *proskuneo*. This word means "to honor your master in humble adoration." It literally means to "kiss toward" or "kiss the hand." It's like the way a dog approaches his master when he has done something wrong. He approaches his master very humbly and respectfully because he is not sure if his behavior has separated him from his master.

Now I'm not calling us dogs, but get the concept. God's love for you goes beyond your behavior. In other words,

God may not love your behavior, but man does He love *you*!

You don't have to cower in humiliation or hide, just acknowledge the offense and come toward God. He will rejoice over you with the pat of forgiveness and the biscuit of a restored relationship.

How does the dog act when he knows the relationship is right again? He's happy and ready for a tail-waggin' good time! Josh Billings says, "A dog is the only thing on earth that loves you more than he loves himself." Now I'm not trying to deify dogs; but, in many ways, wouldn't our community and lives be better if we could adopt a little dog philosophy toward God and others?

••

My goal in life is to be as good of a person as
my dog already thinks I am. −Author unknown

28

Can You Hear Me?

An elderly gentleman of 85 feared his wife was getting hard of hearing. So one day he called her doctor to make an appointment to have her hearing checked. The doctor made an appointment for a hearing test in two weeks. He also suggested a simple, informal test the husband could do to give the doctor some idea of the state of her problem.

"Here's what to do," said the doctor, "start out about 40 feet away from her, and in a normal, conversational speaking tone see if she hears you. If not, go to 30 feet, then 20 feet, and so on until you get a response."

That evening, the wife was in the kitchen cooking dinner and he was in the living room. He thinks, *I'm about 40 feet away, let's see what happens.* In a normal tone, he asks, "Honey, what's for supper?" He gets no response, so he moves to the other end of the room, and repeats, "Honey, what's for supper?" Still no response.

Next he moves to about 20 feet away and asks, "Honey, what's for supper?" Again no response. He walks to only 10 feet away, and still no response. So he walks up right behind her. "Honey, what's for supper?"

"Darn it, Earl, for the fourth time, chicken!"

And my wife says, "Amen."

From time to time, we all can be hard of hearing. That's especially true when we look around the world at people, governments, nations, businesses—the lack of hearing and wisdom and the consequences are becoming more apparent.

Proverbs 24:3-4 states that in order to integrate what is going on around us and to make the best decisions in our situation, we need what I call the three legged stool: knowledge, understanding, and wisdom. Knowledge is *what*, understanding is *why* and wisdom is *how*. Wisdom is the proper application of knowledge through understanding to the benefit of all. Wisdom is bigger than knowledge. Wisdom is proactive, planned, and not reactionary. Wisdom sees and hears the big picture. Wisdom sees that what we do today takes us to tomorrow.

Wisdom says, "Can you hear me?" Wisdom says, "What you are doing today might be legal but is it wise?"

Wisdom is shouting!

"Could what you are doing now, even though you have the right to do it, enslave you later on? Is this profitable for you, your family, and the community in the long run? Does what you are doing now edify yourself and others? Are rights without responsibilities the best course for us in the long run? Is what you are doing now a good example for others?"

....

Can you hear God speaking to you? Are you listening?

29

Life Behind the Curtain

My 16-year-old son Jonathan and I were in Singapore. I was asked to speak at a businessmen's meeting and church meetings. Now let me tell you how I got there. I call it Life Behind the Curtain!

I travel well over 125,000 miles a year speaking at conferences and churches. Most of my flights are with United Airlines because I take advantage of their frequent flyer program.

One of the perks of being a frequent flyer is that I receive system-wide upgrades. You guessed it—Jon and I were upgraded to business class for our trip to Singapore. For the price of a coach-class ticket, we experienced Life Behind the Curtain! As you may know, there is a curtain between coach class and business or first class. Incidentally, Jon will be spoiled the rest of his life!

The experience of flying coach and flying international business is dramatically different. First of all, there is room...lots of room. The seats tilt back to almost horizontal. No problem sleeping on those 12-hour flights. The seats even knead your back while you are sitting or sleeping! The meals are served to you, not thrown at you. You even get three choices of main dishes, the best wine, and great desserts! Let's not forget the six movies playing at the same time on your individual screen. It's a whole new world!

After you experience *this* world, you never want to return to the back of the plane or that *old* world again. I've been known to leave claw marks in the carpet of the plane as they dragged me to the back of the plane when I couldn't be upgraded on flights from Los Angeles to Hong Kong.

Believe it or not, there is a lesson in this high-flying story.

You see, coach class is like our life on earth; business or first class is like our life in Heaven.

Life here on earth is small seats, low ceilings, crowded conditions, paying for edibly-challenged meals, lost baggage, long lines, and security checks. If that's all you have experienced, you think *that* is normal. *That* is as good as it gets.

But as a Christian, I know there is a first-class world waiting for me. It's much better than what I have experienced so far. Talk about perks! It's Life Behind the Curtain for eternity! Even though I love life here on earth, it's nothing compared to the glory that is to be revealed. And the trip was bought and paid for by God through His Son for you and me.

Welcome aboard!

••

Prepare today for your first-class trip into eternity
by praising and worshiping the God in Heaven who made it all possible.

30

Josefina's Secret Weapon

Sometimes your greatest weakness can be your strongest weapon.

The July 19, 1948, edition of *Time* magazine told the astounding story of Josefina Guerrero who was awarded the Medal of Freedom for her heroic partnership with the American government in the face of the harsh brutality of World War II. During the war Joey, as she was called, spied for the Allied forces in Manila in the Philippines.

Joey was young, pretty, and vivacious. Her husband was a wealthy medical student at Santo Tomas University. But after the Japanese invaded the Philippines, she and her friends helped internees and the U.S. prisoners of war—bringing them food, clothing, and medicine. She also carried valuable information back to the U.S. military. She mapped the waterfront areas for the Allied army and prowled the restricted areas recording what she saw. From Joey's drawings, American planes were able to pinpoint their targets. She quickly won the respect and the appreciation of the U.S. officials.

For three years—until the war was over—Joey continued her cloak and dagger career and was never caught. She was stopped several times by suspicious Japanese, but she was never captured or searched because of her secret weapon. What was it? Leprosy!

As a leper she had been an outcast. No one wanted to have anything to do with her. After the war began, the very characteristic that had isolated her from others helped her accomplish her mission. Her weakness became the secret of her strength.

That story comes from author and speaker John Maxwell.[33] Quite a story, huh?

What lessons can we learn from this true story? First of all, don't let what you're *not* affect what you *can be*! In other words, bloom where you are planted. Work with what you have. Look for a way *into* life, not out of it. Look for ways to contribute.

You might think you're too old to do anything, but you can pray! I have a friend who was in jail for eight years. Do you know what he did during that time? He took online classes, studied, and won 31 awards for academic excellence and excellent behavior. He turned the broken eggs of his life into a wonderful omelet!

Second, every person has the potential to add great value. Sometimes it's our weakness that gives us a passport into something significant. God said to the apostle Paul in Second Corinthians, "My strength comes into its own in your weakness." When you stop focusing on your handicap, you can begin appreciating the gifts God has given you!

That's what Josefina did and you can too!

· ·

Consider your secret weapons—take them out, dust them off, and use them to help others at home, at work, in the community, or at church.

31

Fatherly Influence

Being a responsible father in this day and age is especially challenging. J. August Strindberg wrote in his day, "That is the thankless position of the father in the family…the provider for all and the enemy of all." Let me offer an analogy or concept on fathers and mothers that is true in most cases, but not all.

Being a father is like being the police. Being a firefighter is much more popular.

Mom's are like firefighters! Everyone loves them! They rescue you. Father's are seen as the authority figures. They cause us to be responsible. They have teeth! Most mother's nurture—we like that! Most fathers ask questions like, "What are you going to be when you grow up?" Father's have government— we don't like that. Mothers tend to love you no matter what. Fathers still love you but look at results. They like success. Moms are more relational, fathers are more taskers. Both are needed and necessary. God designed families to be win-win, not win-lose!

Now how did Father's Day come into being? It started in the United States. Author Jerry Wilson outlines the beginning.

Sonora Dodd, of Washington, first had the idea of Father's Day. She thought of the idea of Father's Day while listening to a Mother's Day sermon in 1909. Sonora wanted a special day to honor her father, William Smart. Smart, who was a Civil War veteran, was widowed when his wife died after giving birth to their sixth child. Mr. Smart was left to raise the newborn and his other five children by himself on a rural farm in eastern Washington State.

After Sonora became an adult she realized the selflessness her father had shown in raising his children as a single parent. It was her father who made all the parental sacrifices and was, in the eyes of his daughter, a courageous, selfless, and loving man. Sonora's father was born in June, so she chose to hold the first Father's Day celebration in Spokane, Washington, on June 19, 1910.

President Calvin Coolidge, in 1924, supported the idea of a national Father's Day. Then, in 1966, President Lyndon Johnson signed a presidential proclamation declaring the third Sunday of June as Father's Day. President Richard Nixon signed the law that finally made it permanent in 1972.[34]

We all know of not-so-good examples of fathers. It hurts, doesn't it? However, there are many more examples of good fathers. Contact, honor, and thank (or remember) your father soon—even if it's uncomfortable. Police need a little thank you every now and then! Even Sigmund Freud notes, "I cannot think of any need in childhood as strong as the need for a father's protection."

....

Honor your father and your mother, as the Lord your God has commanded you, that your days may be prolonged and that it may go well with you on the land which the Lord your God gives you (**Deuteronomy 5:16**).

32

Prodigals Happen

Whenever your kids are out of control, you can take comfort in the thought that even God's omnipotence did not always extend to His kids. Even the best are sometimes perplexed when it comes to children. Comedian Bill Cosby talks about this in one of his recordings.

After creating Heaven and earth, God created Adam and Eve. The first thing God said to them was: "Don't."

"Don't what?" Adam asked.

"Don't eat the forbidden fruit," said God.

"Forbidden fruit? Really? Where is it?" Adam and Eve asked, jumping up and down excitedly.

"It's over there," said God, wondering why He hadn't stopped after making elephants.

A few minutes later, God saw the kids having an apple break and He was very concerned. "Didn't I tell you not to eat that fruit?" the First Parent asked.

"Uh huh," Adam replied.

"Then why did you do it?" God asked exasperatedly.

"I dunno," Adam answered.

God's punishment was that Adam and Eve should have children of their own.[35]

Through the years, I have worked with parents who have had problems with children. It's only natural that when that happens we tend to blame ourselves.

After all, experience is something you don't get until just after you need it. Then, even after you have experience, there still may be problems.

I once met a missionary couple in India who raised seven children. The first six children were well-adjusted, but the seventh was out of control. The same parenting style, lots of experience, and love were given to all their children but it just didn't work with that seventh child. All the father could do was grieve over that one child. Was it his fault? No and all of us tried to tell him so. Prodigals just happen! The same thing happened to God with Adam and Eve.

I have learned over 26 years of ministry and counseling that almost every prodigal comes home. Sooner or later, just like the prodigal son story in the Bible, there comes a point when children come to their senses. Tired of life in the pig pen, they move slowly back, bruised, and somewhat broken, realizing who their parents are. They come home. And, just like that father in the prodigal son story, we must be waiting on the porch.

That is how God feels about you and me. He didn't move off the porch, we moved away from Him. But He is waiting for you there even now. And He will be as happy about seeing you return to Him as you will be when your prodigal comes home. Come on in...the door is open anytime for His children...and yours!

• •

But the father said to his slaves, "Quickly bring out the best robe and put it on him, and put a ring on his hand and sandals on his feet; and bring the fattened calf, kill it, and let us eat and celebrate; for this son of mine was dead and has come to life again; he was lost and has been found." And they began to celebrate (Luke 15:22-24).

33

Dogs, Cats, Kids, and Teenagers

The story of the Prodigal Son is wonderful encouragement for parents with estranged children. The father never gave up, allowing the process of time to work in his son. Someone wrote this story that gives hope to those struggling through those sometimes tough teen years. It's called "The Cat Years." It's true more often than not.

I just realized that while children seem to be more like dogs—loyal and affectionate— teenagers are more like cats. It's so easy to be a dog owner. You feed it and train it. It puts its head on your knees and gazes at you as if you were a Rembrandt painting. It bounds indoors with enthusiasm when you call it.

Then around age 13 your adorable little puppy turns into a big old cat. When you tell it to come inside it looks amazed, as if wondering who died and made you emperor. Instead of dogging your footsteps, it disappears. You won't see it again until it gets hungry—then it pauses on its sprint through the kitchen to turn its nose up at whatever you're serving.

When you reach out to ruffle its head, it twists away from you, then gives you a blank stare as if trying to remember where it has seen you before. You, not realizing that the dog is now a cat, think something must be desperately wrong with it. It seems so antisocial, so distant, sort of depressed. It won't go on family outings.

Since you're the one who raised it, taught it to fetch, stay, and sit on command, you assume that you did something wrong. Flooded with guilt and fear, you redouble your efforts to make your pet behave. Only now you're dealing with a cat, so everything that worked before now produces the opposite of the desired result. Call it, and it runs away. Tell it to sit, and it jumps on the counter.

Instead of continuing to act like a dog owner, you have to learn to behave like a cat owner. Sit still and it will come, seeking the warm, comfortable lap it has not entirely forgotten.

Be there to open the door for it.

One day your grown-up child walks into the kitchen, gives you a big kiss and says, "You've been on your feet all day, let me get those dishes for you." Then you realize your cat is a dog again.[36]

....

For I am mindful of the sincere faith within you, which first dwelt in your grandmother Lois and your mother Eunice, and I am sure that it is in you as well (2 Timothy 1:5).

34

No Manure—No Milk!

I know what you are thinking. Where did he get that title? Well, I got it from the Book of Proverbs in the Bible. How do you like that? Some people think the Bible is not relevant today. But there is so much wisdom in the Bible, for everyday people like us.

Proverbs 14:4 says, *"Where no oxen are, the manger is clean, but much increase comes by the strength of the ox."* In other words, oxen make a mess but that is better than having clean stalls with no oxen. Remember, in that day and agrarian culture, oxen were like gold. They got things done, plowed the fields, gave milk, hauled the crop to market—the list is long. One trip to India will convince you of the value of oxen.

Where there is life, there will be undesirable stuff from time to time. It's part of life. In order for everything to be perfect, you would have to be a permanent resident of a graveyard! You've seen the bumper sticker, "stuff happens!" Well,

"life happens"

too—both good and bad.

The truth is no person, no government, no country, no city, no marriage, no relationship, no job, no ideology, or no new house is going to be perfect. Those truths are hard ones for us perfectionists to accept! That doesn't mean that we should not strive to make things better. But as they say, the process of life means that stuff happens. If it didn't, we would be dead. Remember, where no oxen are, the manger is clean. No manure, no milk!

Jesus says in Matthew 5:44-45, *"But I say to you, love you enemies, and pray for those who persecute you* [manure] *so that you may be sons of your Father who is in heaven* [milk]; *for He causes his sun to rise on the evil and the good and sends rain on both the righteous and the unrighteous."* You see, no one gets away with all milk and no manure, or all manure and no milk. That's life!

The key to manure is to use it for *growing*, not *groaning!* Too many of us think the light at the end of the tunnel is a train! Some of us, after so many manure experiences, have adopted a defensive attitude of life. You may feel like the guy who went to get his brakes fixed and the mechanic said, "I couldn't repair your brakes, so I made your horn louder!"

Pain in life is inevitable, but misery is optional. The key to life is to enjoy the good times and learn to grow during those not-so-good times. In fact, the bad times in life may produce something wonderful later on. The manure grows the grass that the oxen eat to produce—milk!

Yes, manure happens, stalls get dirty, but at least you're alive!

Got milk?

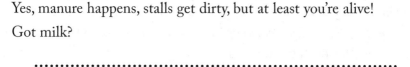

Pain in life is inevitable, but misery is optional.

35

Circumstances—
The Ultimate Joy Robber

Are you struggling with keeping a good attitude and your joy? Is the sound of your own wheels driving you crazy? The Book of Philippians in the Bible warns us of four joy robbers. A different joy robber is identified in each of the four chapters. Author Warren Wiersbe in his book *Be Joyful* points this out.

Let me offer up some thoughts from Philippians about how not to lose your joy and how to recover your joy if you lost it.

First of all, the word *joy* is mentioned 19 times in the Book of Philippians and the word *mind* is mentioned 15 times.

Joy is directly linked to how we think. Joy is determined by how you process what is going on around you.

People may be magnets for misery just by the way they think. The answer? Change your thinking, perspective, and old ways of processing things. How? Let's see how the apostle Paul did it!

Paul identifies *circumstances* in Philippians chapter 1 as the first of the joy robbers. Here is a list of his circumstances as he wrote to the Philippians church. First of all, he was in jail. He was chained to a Praetorian guard, the special operations force of the Roman Empire. These were soldiers from Caesar's very own household. While Paul was in jail, others preachers were preaching Christ for their own gain and being critical of Paul. They were doing this intentionally knowing that it would cause Paul to hurt even more.

Paul was going to give a defense of the Gospel to Nero very soon. This is the emperor who crucified Christians upside down and burned them. On top of that, most all of Paul's friends had left him. The Philippian church members were turning back to their old ways, and falling in an obsessive love with material things. Finally, there were two women in the church who were in quite a fight and were creating factions within the church.

Talk about *circumstances*! That's one big Excedrin headache Paul had to deal with! Now I'm sure there are some of us with bigger problems than Paul's, but not by much. Yet even in the midst of all these *circumstances*, Paul says, "Now I want you to know, brethren, that my *circumstances* have turned out for the greater progress of the gospel" (Phil. 1:12).

In the midst of all his problems, he could see good coming out of it. He wasn't focused on himself. He refused to become a victim. He had a reason for living and that reason for living was being advanced. Knowing this caused him to engage his will and choose to rejoice in the Lord. He was a thermostat, not a thermometer. Thermometers rise and fall with the temperature (circumstances). Thermostats click on the power when the temperature goes up or down.

• •

Now may the God of hope fill you with all joy and peace in believing, so that you will abound in hope by the power of the Holy Spirit (**Romans 15:13**).

36

The Ultimate Joy Robber—
Part II

So apostle Paul was in jail chained to the elite of the Roman soldiers, the Praetorian guard—soldiers from Caesar's own household. Others were intentionally speaking against Paul and speaking for their own gain, knowing that Paul couldn't do anything about it while in jail. On top of that, all of his friends had deserted him.

However, Paul, even in the midst of these circumstances, never loses his joy, perspective, and godly attitude. His circumstances didn't rule him; he ruled his circumstances, or at least his reaction to his circumstances. He was a thermostat, not a thermometer! Thermometers go up and down—they are reactive. Thermostats click on the power for warmth and coolness.

Forced joy is better than genuine depression. The Bible says the joy of the Lord is your strength (see Neh. 8:10). Paul knew that if he lost his joy, he would lose his strength. If you lose your strength, you can't fight. If you can't fight, you will lose the battle of perspective. Paul saw the big picture. He knew there was always, "the rest of the story." He knew that God was up to something redemptive. I call this the "yes...but!"

Yes, he was in jail, but he points out that most of the "brethren" have far more courage to preach the Gospel now that he is in jail. Wow! There's a strategy. Lock up the pastors, and their congregations will start speaking out about the Gospel even more. That's multiplication. Not a bad strategy, unless you are a pastor.

He goes on to tell the Philippians that "all the saints greet you, especially those of Caesar's household" (Phil. 4:22). Get that? The guards were becoming "saints" or Christians. Paul wasn't chained to them. They were chained to Paul. Paul had a captive audience. Those poor soldiers couldn't escape that infectious Christian!

Perhaps you feel like you are chained to a bad circumstance. Maybe it's chained to you.

You can either *go* through it or *grow* through it. Bad circumstances can be strongholds of opportunity.

How? Let God redeem it. Look at the big picture. Paul tells us the secret in Philippians 1:21. "For to me, to live is Christ and to die is gain." What does living mean to you? Money, attention, everything always going your way, a new home? For Paul, to live was Christ first, the circumstances second. This brings a Source and Resource higher than you into the equation. It's more than positive thinking—it is godly living and perspective. The results are peace, perspective, and power beyond life's ups and downs.

· ·

Take control over your circumstances—you are not a victim
when you have God by your side during every step of life's journey.

37

People—
The Second Joy Robber

You've been reading about joy from the Book of Philippians. The first joy robber is being controlled by your *circumstances*. The apostle Paul wrote the Book of Philippians from a jail cell, chained to soldiers, and getting ready to make a defense of the Gospel to the madman Nero. Not exactly good *circumstances!*

In chapter 2 of Philippians Paul introduces us to the second joy robber—*people*. His problem is that he has no one of "kindred spirit" who will be genuinely concerned for the welfare of the church in Philippi in their struggles. It seems that those whom he thought would be of help were not. Why? Because, "they all seek after their own interests, not those of Christ Jesus." (See Philippians 2:20-21.)

Have you ever felt that way?

"I thought I could depend on him, her, or them! Where did they go? Where is their commitment or reliability? They have left me. I thought they were with me." The Bible is relevant for today. Paul was dealing with the same problems you and I deal with!

Many people think: *I can always depend on people. People will make me happy and meet my needs.* Thinking that way is a recipe for a joy meltdown! The truth is, people will let you down—who they are, what they say, and what they do. Don't get me wrong. I'm not people bashing. There are great people in this world, but if your joy is dependent on people meeting your needs all the time, it's not going to happen.

What do you do when you are where Paul was? Do what he did! Remember, Paul always looked for whatever was true, honorable, right, pure, and of good repute. He stopped and thought, got perspective, and saw the big picture. Did it *feel* like there was no one to care for the Philippians or was there *truly* no one who cared?

After getting past the emotion of the moment, he discovered the truth. Yes, many had left him, but not all. There were two partners who were still with him—Timothy and Epaphroditus. He ended up sending Epaphroditus (not a bad name for your next son) to the church in Philippi.

You see, you can choose to focus on the many who have left you, or you can choose focus on those still with you. If you look hard enough, there is usually someone around. It just *feels* like everyone is gone. Besides that, Paul says, you are there for them...they are not there for you. That is considering others more important than yourself. That's the mind of Christ (see Phil. 2:3-7)! Don't use others as a means to your own end.

When Jesus was on earth, He prayed that Peter's faith would not fail. He did not pray that his (or our) pastor, spouse, friend, employer, boyfriend, girl-friend, mayor, etc. would never fail Peter. Keeping your faith and perspective is what is important.

· ·

Don't let those who created yesterday's pain control tomorrow's future!

38

Materialism— The Third Joy Robber

Paul, when writing the Book of Philippians, tells us about four joy robbers. In chapter 1, the joy robber is circumstances. In chapter 2, it is people. The third joy robber, revealed in chapter 3, is material things. The church in Philippi was hungering for material things first and God second. Paul uses the concept of "whose god is their appetite…who set their mind on earthly things" (Phil. 3:19).

That's an interesting concept. What are you hungry for?

There are so many products—each one screaming *"buy me, I will make you happy!"*

If we make *things* the source of our joy, we will be unhappy most of the time. That new dress becomes old, the new, expensive car gets a scratch, the boat becomes an anchor, and your dream house needs repairs. Know what I mean? The Bible doesn't say, "Rejoice in my bank account always and again I say rejoice." The Bible says, "Rejoice in the Lord always." (See Philippians 4:4.)

Now don't get me wrong. Money is good. Material things can be wonderful. However, they aren't designed to give us joy. Money and material things are wonderful servants, but terrible masters. Too many people in today's world have made money their master, their purpose, and their aim. They are driven to accumulate. They have become material men and women.

The assumption they make is that material things will give them security and make them happy. The truth is, material things will let us down and fade away. As we seek to possess things, they can end up possessing us and putting us under bondage. Money is a servant, the love of money is a master. You can have money, but money should never have you. The same is true for material things.

"for the kingdom of God is not eating and drinking, but righteousness and peace and joy in the Holy Spirit" (Romans 14:17).

Apostle Paul is encouraging us and the Philippians to handle accumulation with care. It's dangerous stuff—it can rob you of joy. It's the means to an end, not the end itself. His encouragement to the Philippians and us is to make the *Treasurer* (God) our pleasure and not the *treasure*. Seek first the Kingdom of God and the treasure will take care of itself. That's joy! That's life! That's *living!*

. . . .

What are you hungry for? Satisfy your appetite once and for all by serving up a generous portion of God's Kingdom of righteousness, peace, and joy.

39

Worry —
The Fourth Joy Robber

While shopping at a local mall, I noticed a Native American woman wearing a shirt that said, "Don't worry...be Hopi!" I like that, and it brings us to the last robber the apostle Paul writes about in the Book of Philippians—worry.

Paul writes to these very worried people in the church at Philippi, *"Don't worry...be happy!"* He encourages them in Philippians chapter 4, verses 6 and 7, "Don't fret or worry. Instead of worrying, pray. Let petitions and praises shape your worries into prayers, letting God know your concerns. Before you know it, a sense of God's wholeness, everything coming together for good, will come and settle you down. It's wonderful what happens when Christ displaces worry at the center of your life." These verses are from The Message, a translation of the Bible.

Do you realize that 92 percent of what we worry about never happens? The idea behind the Greek word Paul uses for *worry* means "to strangle." Worry can strangle you, paralyze you, make small things appear large, and large things even larger.

In a general sense, worry is more destructive than constructive.

Worry makes it hard to focus. Worry can strangle your good sense at the time when you need perspective the most. Worry makes you reactive rather than proactive. In short, worry can take control—*quickly.*

Worry is wrong thinking which comes from the mind, and wrong feeling which comes from the heart. It is the result of the first three joy robbers. Worry is wrong thinking and wrong feeling about circumstances, people, and material things. It comes from the assumption that we can depend on circumstances, people, and material things to get us through life. But in reality, the worry button in us is clicked on by circumstances, people, and the love of material things.

Changing your source of joy changes your life. With Christ at the center of your life, you change your source of joy. Let God displace worry in your life. The Kenyans call this Hakunaah Matata!

God has it under control. There's nothing too big for Him. The Bible tells us, "I can do all things through Christ who strengthens me" (Phil. 4:13 NKJV). That's good advice for the *worry challenged*. This was good advice for the Philippines then and it is good advice for us today.

I'll take joy over worry any day. How about you?

· ·

Hakunaah Matata!

40

Socrates and the Turkey Carcass

In the United States, the first holiday of the "holiday season" is Thanksgiving. Thanksgiving is celebrated to remember the time when the Pilgrims gave thanks to God for their first harvest. It is also the time when extended families get together and have a Thanksgiving meal. Allow me to share a Thanksgiving with you that happened when I was a youngster.

In 1962, in Phoenix, Arizona, I was 13 years old and dinosaurs were still roaming the earth. Just kidding. It was the first Thanksgiving in our new home, and Thanksgiving was a big deal! All of the Delph clan would assemble, and enjoy the coveted Thanksgiving turkey meal prepared by my mother who is the best cook on earth. Aunts, uncles, grandparents, heaps of cousins, my siblings and parents were all present. And so was our favorite dog and family mascot, Socrates.

Socrates was a gigantic standard dachshund, the original model that wasn't bred down to the size of a hot dog. He looked more like a black and tan basset hound. The thing I remember most about Socrates was his appetite. This dog lived to eat, and he would eat almost anything.

Well, the Thanksgiving dinner was finished, and everyone was in the living room. The perfect scenario for a hungry dog in stealth mode. Somehow Socrates ascended to the heights of the kitchen counter and clapped onto the remains of the 25-pound turkey.

Before I tell you the end of the story, let's imagine what Socrates was thinking.

I know what day this is—Thanksgiving. My family is thanking me for being such a good dog! They are thanking me for the robbers I have chased off, and the miles I have walked on this mountain with cactus scratching my belly. They are thanking me for raising three children. I better find a safe place to eat this bountiful reward. I know, I'll eat this culinary miracle under Ed's bed. I better go quickly. I don't want to lose any of that juice that's leaking out of this lovely carcass. What a Thanksgiving! What a reward! I'm sooooooo doggon thankful!

Needless to say Socrates was discovered by following the grease trail on Mom's new white carpet. Socrates put up a valiant effort to keep his treasure. As I recall, that was the only time he ever bit Dad.

What a fond memory that became for family and friends and those who are not with us anymore. When Thanksgiving rolls around at your house this year, try not to focus on what you don't have. Focus on what you have, and be thankful. The Scripture says in First Thessalonians 5:18, "In everything give thanks for this is God's will for you in Christ Jesus."

Oh by the way, when Socrates went to sleep that Thanksgiving evening, I bet he was thinking, *I wonder what I'll get for Christmas!*

....

Allow good memories to keep you warm in the winter of life,
and smiling during the other seasons.

41

When We're Too Busy to Be Busy

A little girl, dressed in her Sunday best, was running as fast as she could, trying not to be late for Sunday school class. As she ran she prayed, "Dear Lord, please don't let me be late! Dear Lord, please don't let me be late!" While she was running and praying, she tripped on the curb and fell, getting her clothes dirty and tearing her dress.

She got up, brushed herself off, and started running again. As she ran, she once again began to pray. "Dear Lord, please don't let me be late...but please, don't push me either!"[37]

It's easy to go too fast in today's world, isn't it? I think it starts while you are a teenager. Life gets busy. From there it just seems to get busier. Marriage, children, careers, sports, and then you are dealing with teenagers again! This time, it's *their* schedule, not yours! They tell me life is supposed to slow down, but my parents are still going like crazy...and I was born in 1949. It's easy to feel like that little girl in the story, "Dear Lord, please don't let me be late...but don't push me either!"

Life can be less frantic if we learn a lesson from a robot. No, not the kind of robot you are thinking of. In South Africa, they call traffic control lights, robots. Every traffic light has three colors; green, yellow, and red. Just like robots, people have green, yellow, and red times in life. Sometimes, we go—green. Sometimes, we need to slow down and proceed cautiously—yellow. Then there are those red-light times when we are stopped but others can go.

There are other people in the universe, right? Surely, someone else can have a turn, can't they?

What I get concerned about in my life are those yellow and red times.

I exceed in the green times. After all, I live in the 21ˢᵗ century! But what if the times call for a little more of a cautious approach to life? Should I keep spending extravagantly when the economy is down? Should I be gone all the time when my teenagers are struggling and need me? Should I keep working all the time when my body, like the warning light on my dashboard, says slow down?

What do you do during a busy time in life when the robot is flashing yellow? My advice, slow down. Conducting your life in a yellow light time in a green light way can be dangerous to you and others around you. You may even trip and, just like that little girl, blame the Lord, "...don't push me!"

· ·

To keep your traffic control light working properly, take time to access the traffic patterns and choose wisely when to go, proceed cautiously, or stop!

42

A Bear of Prayer

Two missionaries agree, just before they leave for the missions field, that once a year they will get together to go hunting on the first day of deer season. For several years this had taken place. Their wives became best of friends and also looked forward to the traditional annual hunt.

One year, the two hunters were whistling a merry tune while in the woods and came upon a very large bear enjoying berries. The bear heard them, raised himself up to see better and turned to move toward them.

"What do we do?"

"Shoot it!"

"We can't! Bears are protected in this area—the fine is $10,000."

"Then RUN!"

They headed for the woods for protection. They could hear the deep panting of the bear gaining on them with every breath.

"What should we do?"

"Pray!"

They both stopped in their tracks and spoke the following prayer. "Father in Heaven, please make this bear a Christian. Amen!"

Then the bear stopped dead in his tracks.

The two missionaries could not hear the bear any longer. They slowly turned around to see the bear kneeling on the ground with his massive arms folded in quiet reverence. Then they heard a groan from the bear that sounded like: "Father in Heaven, bless this food that I am about to partake. Amen."[38]

I once heard someone say,

"God answers prayer in three ways—yes, no, and you've got to be kidding!" I think it's more like yes, no, slow, or grow.
The Bible says that God is a God who answers prayer. I believe that. I have to trust that Father knows best.

Missionary Hudson Taylor first went to China in a sailing vessel. As the ship neared the shore of cannibal islands, the wind stopped. The ship drifted toward the shore, much to the delight of the stomachs of the island's inhabitants.

The ship's captain came to Rev. Taylor and begged him to pray for the help of God. "I will," said Taylor, "provided you set your sails to catch the breeze." The captain declined to make himself a laughing stock by unfurling in the dead calm. Taylor said, "I will not undertake to pray for the vessel unless you will prepare your sails." And it was done.

While engaged in prayer, there was a knock at the door of his stateroom. "Who is there?" The captain responded, "Are you still praying for wind?"

"Yes."

"Well," said the captain, "you'd better stop praying, for we have more wind than we can manage."[39]

Never underestimate the power of prayer. I'm so glad that Hudson Taylor didn't pray for those cannibals to be Christians...at least not then!

••

...The effective prayer of a righteous man can accomplish much (James 5:16).

43

A Pledge of Quality and Satisfaction

I'd like to share two prayers with you. Here's the first. "Dear Lord, so far today I've done all right. I haven't gossiped, haven't lost my temper, haven't been greedy, grumpy, nasty, selfish, or overindulgent. I'm very thankful for that. But, in a few minutes, Lord, I'm going to get out of bed. And, from then on, I'm probably going to need a lot more help. Amen."[40]

Now, I think most of us can relate to this prayer, can't we? Like anything else, Christianity is much easier to preach than to live, isn't it? It's easy to go to church. It's hard to be the church. It's easy to read the Bible. It's much harder to live the Bible.

The inconsistency of knowing and living Christianity is what drives others crazy.

That's why Christians are often called hypocrites.

Now, here is the second prayer. It's written by an unknown author. The prayer is somewhat preachy but makes some great points about living out the Lord's Prayer. I'll capitalize the Lord's Prayer as you read. "I cannot say OUR if my religion has no room for others and their needs. I cannot say FATHER if I do not demonstrate this relationship in my daily living. I cannot say WHO ART IN HEAVEN if all my interests and pursuits are earthy things.

I cannot say HALLOWED BE THY NAME if I, called by His name, have no integrity. I cannot say THY KINGDOM COME if I am unwilling to give up my own sovereignty and accept His. I cannot say THY WILL BE DONE if I am unwilling or resentful of having it in my life. I cannot say ON EARTH AS IT IS IN HEAVEN unless I am truly ready to give myself to His service here and now.

I cannot say GIVE US THIS DAY OUR DAILY BREAD without extending honest effort for it or by ignoring the genuine needs of my fellow human. I cannot say FORGIVE US OUR TRESPASSES AS WE FOR-GIVE THOSE WHO TRESPASS AGAINST US if I continue to hold a grudge against anyone. I cannot say LEAD US NOT INTO TEMPTA-TION BUT DELIVER US FROM EVIL if I am not prepared to live and fight for what is good through prayer, choice, and lawful action.

I cannot say THINE IS THE KINGDOM if I do not give the King my utmost for His highest. I cannot say THINE IS THE POWER if I fear what others think about me when my behavior is humane and godly. I can-not say THINE IS THE GLORY if I am seeking my own glory first by using spiritual things. I cannot say FOREVER if I am too anxious or wor-ried by daily matters. And I cannot say AMEN unless I honestly say....*come what may, this is my prayer.*"

Now, there's a challenge for us. And, I might say, we are all works in progress. Can we give one another a little grace about this? And, besides, if a hypocrite is standing between you and God, the hypocrite is closer to God than you are—think about it.

• •

In Jesus' name…

44

Mountain or Mole Hill?

Little Davie watched, fascinated, as his mother smoothed cold cream on her face. "Why do you do that, Mommy?" he asked.

"To make myself beautiful," said his mother who then began removing the cream with a tissue.

"What's the matter," asked little Davie, "giving up?"

You may feel like quitting. You may feel like giving up. You feel lower than a snake's belly. I understand, I've been there too. I'll try not to be too shallow in addressing this issue. Most times when you feel like quitting, changing your emotional scenery helps. Remember, we walk through the valley of the shadow of death, not camp in it. God believes in you, and doesn't want you to give up.

Do you realize that mountains are in the eyes of the beholder? Some see a mountain as a mole hill. Others see a mol ehill as a mountain. Sometimes we don't need to be holding what we are beholding. As I'm writing, my son Jon is pointing out that he is not quite sure if what I'm saying is true. He's says he has seen some mighty big mountains! Haven't we all? However, I'm not sure I want doubt as my best friend in times of trouble.

I tend to be more positive, because I don't like the alternative.

Have you ever had a resume rejected? The next time a nasty rejection letter comes your way, respond with your own:

Dear [Interviewer's Name]:[41]

Thank for your letter of [date]. After careful consideration, I regret to inform you that I am unable to accept your refusal to offer me employment with your firm. This year I have been particularly fortunate in receiving an unusually large number of rejection letters. With such a varied and promising field of candidates, it is impossible for me to accept all the refusals.

Despite your outstanding qualifications and previous experience in rejecting applicants, I find that your rejection does not meet with my needs at this time. Therefore, I will initiate employment with your firm beginning on [xx/xx/xxxx]. I look forward to seeing you then. Best of luck in rejecting future candidates. Sincerely...

Now, there's new one for you! But in those times sullen times of doubt and quitting, avoid words and phrases like "I can't, I'm afraid of, I don't think so, maybe, if only, I don't have time, it's impossible, I don't believe, I doubt if I, and I wish I had." Words like those often create bleak and barren emotional scenery that only make matters worse.

Instead, choose words that jump start you to turning mountains into mole hills. Words and phrases such as, "I can, I'm confident I can, I know so, positively, I will, I will make time, with God it is possible, I believe, I expect the best, and I'm happy with what I have," are very helpful. While these words may not change your circumstances, they change your attitude. That's half the battle!

....

After all, the Bible says in Philippians 4:13, "I can do all things through Him who strengthens me." And that was written for some people going through some really rough times.

45

Blogging Fried Eggs

A wife was making a breakfast of fried eggs for her husband. Suddenly her husband burst into the kitchen. "Careful," he said, "CAREFUL! Put in some more butter! Oh my God! You're cooking too many at once. TOO MANY! Turn them! TURN THEM NOW! We need more butter. Oh my God! Where are we going to get more butter? They're going to stick! Careful...CAREFUL! I said be CAREFUL!

"You never listen to me when you're cooking! Never! Turn them! Hurry up! Are you CRAZY? Have you lost your mind? Don't forget to salt them. You know you always forget to salt them. Use the salt. USE THE SALT! THE SALT! THE SALT!"

The wife stared at him. "What in the world is wrong with you? You think I don't know how to fry a couple of eggs?"

The husband calmly replied, "I wanted you to hear what it's like when I'm driving."[42]

I can feel the tension on that one! Men will use this story as ammunition all over the world. However, many men give the opposite sex lots of ammunition to use! My wife, Becky, tells me that all the time. There, you see, I've been fair to all parties!

What's the lesson? Today's world has become a world where critics rule. It's popular to micromanage. Just listen to radio talk shows, read blog sites, and read news that is fact made in opinion's image. It's popular to build yourself up by tearing others down. It's a world where you find fault with others before looking at yourself.

Many folks are like the crowd in a stadium. They watch, they criticize, they critique, and they reject. The only time audiences like this are satisfied is when everything and everyone is perfect. That happens rarely!

God warned us against this type of fault-finding attitude. He knew that it would produce a multitude of fruit inspectors and fruit eaters. He knew that it would eventually choke out the fruit *bearers* everyone needs. In a fault-finding environment, it doesn't take long before the fruit bearers begin shrink into mediocrity.

Why take a risk? Why stand out? Why excel when everything you do will be micromanaged by the so-called experts.

Do you remember the story in John chapter 21 when Peter looks at John and says to Jesus, "What about this man?" Jesus said to Peter the fruit inspector, "…What is that to you? You follow Me!" In other words, Jesus was saying, "…*mind your own business! Peter, look at me, not him!*" Now, there's good advice. Focusing on Jesus will keep your soul clean, improve your attitude, and even put a smile on your face.

You can tell how big people are by what it takes to make them critical. Isn't it time to affirm who others are, not point out what they are not?

....

Look for the good in people—and the favor will be returned.

46

Don't Just Go for It, Sow for It!

Here's a story that makes quite a point on the subject of sowing and reaping. Read on and fasten your seat belts!

Married for 25 years, he looked at his wife one day and said, "Honey, 25 years ago, we had a cheap apartment, an old car, we slept on a sofa bed, and watched a 10-inch black and white television—but I got to sleep every night with a hot, 25-year-old blonde. Now, we have a nice house, a new car, a big bed, and a plasma screen television, but I'm sleeping with a 50-year-old woman. It seems to me that you are not holding up your side of things."

His wife was a very reasonable woman. She said, "Well, go out and find yourself a hot, 25-year-old blonde, and I'll make sure that you will once again have a cheap apartment, an old car, sleep on a sofa bed, and watch a 10-inch black and white television."

Actions have consequences. The wife's reaction illustrates my point. Many people today don't think about consequences. They just do what they want to do and then are surprised when the reaping comes. How many have learned the hard way that seat belts are not as confining as wheelchairs? How many have learned the hard way that a good time to keep your mouth shut is when you are in deep water?

The Bible says in Galatians 6:7, "Do not be deceived, God is not mocked; for whatever a man sows, this he will also reap."

There is a principle of sowing and reaping.

This principle is at work in everything we do. We can either use this principle or be used by this principle. We can use it to produce positive results or negative results. It depends on what kind of seed we sow.

Let's become aware of this fact of life and activate it for our benefit, for our family's benefit, and for the benefit of our communities. With the help of this principle, we may even improve our dog's lives! Money will buy a fine dog, but kindness will make him wag his tail.

....

The nicest thing about the future is that it always starts today.

47

Three Laws of
Sowing and Reaping

An amateur genealogical researcher discovered that his great great uncle, Remus Starr, a fellow lacking in character, was hung for horse stealing and train robbery in Montana in 1889. The only known photograph of Remus shows him standing on the gallows. On the back of the picture is the following inscription. "Remus Starr; horse thief; sent to Montana Territorial Prison 1885; escaped 1887; robbed the Montana Flyer train six times. Caught by Pinkerton Detectives. Convicted and hanged in 1889."

In a family history, subsequently written by the researcher, Remus's picture is cropped so that all that is seen is a head shot. The accompanying biographical sketch was as follows: "Remus Starr was a famous cowboy in the Montana Territory. His business empire grew to include the acquisition of valuable equestrian assets and intimate dealings with the Montana railroad. Beginning in 1885, he devoted several years of his life to service in a government facility, finally taking leave to resume his dealings with the railroad. In 1887, he was a key player in a vital investigation run by the renowned Pinkerton Detective Agency. In 1889, Remus passed away during an important civic function held in his honor when the platform upon which he was standing collapsed."

At times, that sounds like how our mainline media report stories today, doesn't it? The Bible says in Galatians 6:7, "Do not be deceived, God is not mocked; for whatever a man sows, this he will also reap." Most of what we do in life is really just sowing seeds and reaping the harvest of those seeds. The seeds we sow can be our attitudes, our choices, our words, our time spent with family or friends, our money, our care and concern or lack thereof. Harvests come from these seeds that can work for or against us.

Now let's talk about the three laws of sowing and reaping.

Law #1: *You reap what you sow.* If you plant an apple seed, you will get an apple tree, unless it's been nuked, cloned, or grafted in some way. In other words, if you desire a friend, you sow friendship to others. The best vitamin for friendship is B-1. If you desire compassion, be compassionate yourself. If you want forgiveness, forgive others. You sow first and reap second.

Law #2: *You reap more than you sow.* One kernel of corn can produce thousands of kernels of corn.

One kind act in the community by you can touch thousands of others.

Conversely, one destructive act, can adversely affect thousands. The Bible says in Hosea 8:7, "For they sow the wind, and they reap the whirlwind...." One little match can destroy an entire forest.

Law #3: *You reap later than you sow.* Seeds take time to grow. Some plants grow quickly, others take years to mature. What we think we are getting away with today, may just come back to visit us tomorrow—like Remus Starr. Conversely, if you are investing and planting good things, don't get discouraged. The Bible says you will reap if you don't get weary.

···

What goes around, comes around—make sure what's going around
is something you want to encounter again.

48

Change a Bad Harvest into a Good Harvest

For those of you going through rough times in your lives caused by past choices or sowings and who want a better future, there is a way to make that happen. As you read previously, the nicest thing about the future is that it always starts today.

Let's look at some wisdom from Grandpa, an expert in sowing and reaping significant relationships.

"Whether a man winds up with a nest egg or a goose egg, depends a lot on the kind of chick he marries. Trouble in marriage often starts when a man gets so busy earnin' his salt that he forgets his sugar. When a man marries a women, they become one; but the trouble starts when they try to decide which one! If a man has enough horse sense to treat his wife like a thoroughbred, she will never turn into an old nag. On anniversaries, the wise husband always forgets the past, but never the present."[43]

Now here's the secret to overcoming bad harvests:

In the midst of a negative harvest, start to plant good seeds.

For example, if you have been unfaithful in the past and are now paying the price for it, be faithful in the present. If you have been judgmental and bitter in the past, be understanding and forgiving in the present. If you have been unmerciful in the past, be merciful in the present. If you have been stingy to others in the past, be more generous in the present. If you have a habit of lying, start now to sow seeds of telling the truth.

What does it take to start sowing good seed? First of all, it takes a revelation of the truth of what the Bible says about sowing and reaping to the point of trusting and acting on it. Then it involves taking responsibility for your destructive sowing in the past. It takes a truth encounter. It takes forgiveness of others and yourself. Forgiveness makes the future possible.

It takes resources higher than you. It takes God to give you the power to transform your life by transforming your mind and the way you have lived your life in the past. It takes becoming aware of others and what your actions do to others positively or negatively. It takes looking at people and circumstances through grace-healed eyes.

Why not start sowing good seed in the form of attitudes, actions, and understanding to others? It's a win for you, others, and your community. And, by the way, please don't think, "Oh I wish so and so was here to read this." It's written for you and me, not them.

....

If it's going to be, it starts with me and a little wisdom from Grandpa!

49

Hidden Realities

According to a radio report, the administrators in a middle school in Oregon were faced with a unique problem. A number of girls were beginning to use lipstick and they would put it on in the school's restrooms. That was fine, but after they put on their lipstick, they would press their lips to the mirrors—by the end of the day there were dozens of little lip prints covering the mirrors.

Finally, the principal decided that something had to be done. She called all the girls to the restroom and met them there with the custodian. She explained that all these lip prints were causing a major problem for the custodian who had to clean the mirrors every day.

To demonstrate how difficult it was to clean the mirrors, she asked the custodian to clean one. He took out a long-handled brush, dipped it into the nearest toilet and scrubbed the mirror. Since then there have been no lip prints on the mirrors.

I wonder if we would continue doing some things if we knew they were dangerous. The girls were unaware of the mouthful of germs they were getting each time they kissed the mirror. After they realized the danger, they stopped the behavior.

God wants us to avoid a mouthful of germs—sin. Sin means missing the mark of what gives us long-term health and quality of life. Sin is not hurtful because it is forbidden; it is forbidden because it is hurtful! It's truth or consequences in its truest form. It's also God's love proven to us in its purest form.

Have you noticed that opportunity may knock once, but temptation bangs on your door forever? God gave us a conscience to warn us of potential trouble. Conscience is what hurts when everything else feels so good.

Our affections can determine our destiny. The problem is that small things can quickly turn into large, untamable beasts. Emotions and lust end up controlling us. That which is at first weak overcomes the strong. Larger forces often lie behind weaker forces—like those toilet germs. Businessman Warren Buffett said, "Chains of habit are too light to be felt until they are too heavy to be broken."[44]

Please realize that God wants us to have freedom *from*, not just freedom *to*! Many people need freedom *from* drugs, not just freedom *to* drugs. God wants us to have freedom from disabling addictions, although He gives you a free will to choose.

Sin is not about limiting your freedoms, it's about choosing wisely and trusting God.

....

The hidden reality? There just may be some germs on that mirror!

50

Content on the
Inside and Outside

Two show stallions are arguing over who should take best of breed. The first stallion says, "I'll grant you that you are the closest I have ever seen to my equal, but my legs are just a bit straighter than yours, and you know the legs are of prime importance. No foot, no horse!"

The second horse says, "I'll allow that your legs are just a bit better than mine, but mine are the legs I was born with. I know for a fact you had thousands of dollars of corrective work. Your foals will inherit your natural legs, not your genius farrier!"

The first horse mulls this for a moment and then says, "You're right. I stand corrected."[45]

I couldn't resist that one!

But there is quite a message in this story. These are the days of plastic surgery, liposuction, augmentations, enhancements, and cosmetic surgery. One can spend thousands of dollars not just looking good but trying to look perfect on the outside. Like that stallion, they stand corrected.

Don't get me wrong, I think there can be value in some "improvements." But what about the *inside* of the person?

If your soul is out of sorts, it will leak to your outside—no matter how much surgery you've had.

How do you make a person beautiful and peaceful on the inside? How do you do cosmetic surgery on the soul? It starts with living from being loved, not for being loved. It starts with living from being secure, not for being secure. It starts with living from significance, not living for significance. Searching for significance is the ruin of many a man and woman.

Inner peace and beauty comes from knowing God. "Jesus, *knowing* that the Father had given all things into His hands, and that He had come forth from God, and was going back to God" (John 13:3). Jesus knew who He was and was content with it. He didn't need to prove anything. He came from God and was going back to God. No fear of the future. No search for significance. No fear of being rejected. No mind games. No desperate need to be noticed. Living from being loved, not for being loved.

He was content on the inside. That inner contentment radiated from the inside out because of God. As a result, Jesus could serve others rather than be obsessed with Himself. So who do you go to to receive soul surgery? To the Great Physician, of course! God makes house calls. He also hangs out at most local churches. While church members may not all be perfect, it's still God's primary office residence for long-lasting, effective, soul surgery. After all, everyone wants to be well, both in body *and* soul!

....

**Do more than just stand corrected—be content knowing
that you are a perfect child of God.**

51

Pastors' Night Out

A few weeks ago, the local baseball team in our area, the Arizona Diamondbacks, hosted an open house for about 350 pastors in our city. We sat in the special suites, ate snacks, drank soft drinks, and watched a great baseball game. It was like a pastors' night out—but baseball rather than bunco! After all, ladies have nights out! Sports fanatics have nights out! Why can't pastors have nights out?

I was talking about the baseball event to one of my friends. He seemed very intrigued. Finally, he asked me, "What do pastors talk about when they have nights out?" Interesting, huh? He knew what the bingo, bunco, baseball, bowling, and American Idol crowds talk about. But, what do pastors talk about?

Well, as a pastor, I can tell you that pastors are human and have fun too. Yes, we talk about church stuff, but most of us also love humor. I heard some great stories that night. All in good fun! Here's a free pass into our kind of humor.

A visiting minister was very long-winded. Worse yet, every time he made a good point during his sermon and a member of the congregation responded with "Amen" or "That's right, preacher," he would get more wound up and launch into another lengthy discourse. Finally, the host preacher started responding to every few sentences with "Amen, Pharaoh!" The guest minister wasn't sure what that meant, but after several more "Amen, Pharaohs!" he finally concluded his very lengthy discourse.

After the service concluded and the congregation was gone, the visiting minister turned to his host and asked, "What exactly did you mean when you said, 'Amen, Pharaoh'"?

His host replied, "I was telling you to let my people go!"

Every pastor and congregation member can relate to that.

Here's another story. My pastor friend put sanitary hot-air hand dryers in the restrooms at his church. However, after two weeks he took the dryers out. I asked him why, and he confessed that one day he went into the restroom and saw a sign that read, "For a sample of this week's sermon, push the button." Ouch!

One more story, OK? The poor Beartown pastor was livid when he confronted his wife with a receipt for $225 for a new dress.

"What made you do this?" he exclaimed.

"I don't know" she wailed. "I was standing in the store looking at the dress. Then I found myself trying it on. It was like the devil was whispering to me, 'Wow, you look great in that dress. You should buy it!'"

"Well," the pastor persisted, "you know how to deal with him! Just say, 'Get behind me, satan!'"

"I did," replied the wife, "but then he said, 'It looks great from back here, too!'"

You see, pastor's are human too. We even know some good jokes.

And, we would love to share some humor with you—at church!

• •

Try on church this week—it may just be a perfect fit!

52

A Cool Spirit in Hot Times

I don't know about you but certain places and situations make me nervous. For example, speaking in front of politicians or taking a final examination which determines whether you graduate or not. How about wrestling with a computer? But the worst, as far as I'm concerned, is being cross-examined by lawyers in a court room. Those folks can make black look white, true seem false, and good seem evil quicker than my 20-year-old son can devour a candy bar. You have to keep your cool in hot times like those.

If you ever have to testify in court, you might take a lesson on being cool from this story about a very sharp policeman who was being cross-examined by a defense attorney trying to undermine the policeman's credibility.

"Officer—did you see my client fleeing the scene?"

"No sir. But I subsequently observed a person matching the description of the offender running several blocks away."

"Officer—who provided the description?"

"The officer who responded to the scene."

"A fellow officer provided the description of this so-called offender. Do you trust your fellow officers?"

"Yes, sir. With my life."

"With your life? Let me ask you this question then, officer. Do you have a room where you change your clothes in preparation for your daily duties?"

"Yes sir, we do."

"And do you have a locker in your room?"

"Yes sir, I do."

"And do you have a lock on your locker?"

"Yes sir."

"Now why is it, officer, if you trust your fellow officers with your life, you find it necessary to lock your locker in a room you share with these fellow officers?"

"Well, you see, sir, we share the building with the court complex, and sometimes lawyers have been known to walk through that room."[46]

Now please don't be offended if you're a lawyer. Here's the lesson—one of my favorite Bible verses, "He who restrains his words has knowledge, and He who has a *cool spirit* is a man of understanding" (Prov. 17:27).

I like that concept of having a *cool spirit*.

That policeman possessed a cool spirit during a hot time.

Jesus had that same spirit. The lawyers and religious leaders of His time were trying everything they knew to catch Him in a lie or some legal technicality. Yet, time after time, He remained calm, cool, and collected. He wasn't intimidated. He was proactive, not reactive. He had control of His spirit. His mind was in charge, not his emotions.

Your mind and God's power can get you through anger, fear, disappointment, and intimidation. Don't just go through it, with God's ennoblement, *grow* though it! Remember the Proverb of the cool spirit. This even works on the golf course!

• •

A cool spirit is the main ingredient for a refreshing situation.

53

Reflections of a New Grandfather

Well, this week I became a grandfather. A few years ago I instructed my daughter and her husband not to have a baby just yet. The reason? I wasn't old enough! But after seeing little Madeleine Grace, all 6 pounds 3 ounces of her, I have decided that I am now old enough. Wow! My daughter birthing a daughter. It seems as if only a few years ago she was *our* little baby! Now, both my little girl and *her* little girl are beautiful, heavenly, and just as perfect as can be! Just ask any father or grandparent. They will tell you.

Madeleine Grace makes up for all those AARP mailings.

Madeleine Grace makes up for the expensive health insurance at grandparent age. Why, after seeing Madeleine Grace, I even feel good enough to order from the Senior's Menu at Denny's.

For the months leading up to Madeleine's birth, I had been obsessed about what she will call me. Granddad? Sounds a little old to me. Grandfather? That's too distinguished. Grandpa? No, that doesn't work—too old fashioned. Fine for others but not for me.

On one of my international speaking tours, I asked my Hong Kong hosts what the word for grandfather is in Chinese. "Kong…kong!" That name has the idea of respect with it. I love the concept but it sounds too close to King Kong. I'm no King Kong. My nose is too long!

My children have always called my father and their grandfather Pop Pop. I love that name. It was the name my father called his grandfather. But, what would my children call my Dad now if I was Pop Pop. Great Pop Pop? Do you see the stress I was under? I need to have the perfect name for someone as perfect as Madeleine Grace.

So for the moment, I have decided on Opa. Not the fish from Hawaii. Opa is German for grandfather. There's even a Website that sells a coffee cup with "Bester Opa Der Welt" printed on it. That means the "Best Grandpa in the World." Now that's impressive! Also, *opa* in Greek means "joy." So, I'll be a joyful grandfather.

Madeleine means "one who is elevated, a high tower, or a tower of strength." *Grace* means "favor, blessing, and graceful." Grace is a virtue name referring to God's grace. Her nickname will be Ellie from Mad-El-eine. *Ellie* means "light, bright one." Ellie is actually a familiar derivative of Helen which was an unintentional but happy discovery. Helen was my daughter's maternal great grandmother's name.

So, there you have it. I have a granddaughter who is light, bright, has favor and blessing, a graceful one who is elevated, a strong and high tower, and has a perfect nose like Opa! I told you she is perfect!

••

For the Lord is good; His lovingkindness is everlasting and His faithfulness to all generations (Psalm 100:5).

54

The Acknowledgment Section

As my 5-year-old son and I were headed to McDonald's one day, we passed a car accident. Usually, when we see something terrible like that, we say a prayer for those who might be hurt. I said to my son, "We should pray." From the back seat I heard his earnest request: "Please, God, don't let those cars block the entrance to McDonald's."

Now that's reality! Nothing improves our prayer life like a good reason to pray. When confronted with something we have no control over, man, do we get spiritual.

There are worse things than getting a wrong number call at 4 A.M. It could be the right number!

I imagine that's happened to you too. To many, prayer is like the National Anthem at a sports game. It's a nice opening, a formality, like prayer before dinner. Others may look at prayer as a kind of rabbit's foot you pull out and rub when things are tough. Sound familiar? Of course it does!

But what happens when God answers our prayers? What happens when, in spite of our obvious lack of prayer unless the occasion or crisis precipitates it, He answers our prayer?

I received the following story from a friend.

I dreamed that I went to Heaven and an angel was showing me around. We walked inside a large workroom filled with angels. The angel stopped in front of the first section and said, "This is the Receiving Section. Here, all the petitions to God in prayer are received." I looked around and this area was very busy with many angels sorting out petitions written on thousands, maybe millions, of paper sheets and scraps from people all around the world.

Then we moved down a long corridor until we reached the second section. The angel said, "This is the Packing and Delivery Section. Here, the petitions and blessings are processed and delivered to those who asked for them." Again, I noticed how busy it was. There were many angels working hard in this section since so many blessings had been requested and were being packaged for delivery on Earth.

Finally, at the farthest end of the long corridor, we stopped at the door of a very small section. To my great surprise, only one angel was seated there, idly doing nothing. "This is the Acknowledgment Section," my angel friend said. The angel seemed embarrassed.

"How is it that there is no work going on here?" I asked.

"It's sad," the angel sighed. "after people receive the blessings and answers to the prayers they asked for, very few send back acknowledgments."

"How does one acknowledge God's blessings?" I asked.

"Simple," the angel answered. "Just say, 'Thank you, Lord!'"

While I realize that some of us haven't had our prayers answered the way we would have liked, wouldn't it be good to acknowledge the times when God has answered? You would want the same treatment, wouldn't you? Remember, when we work, we work. When we pray, God works, and that is something to be thankful for!

· ·

God answers each and every prayer—maybe not exactly how you thought He would, but He answers them all the same. Take time to thank Him for His loving-kindness.

55

The Person or the Package?

For years a huge, ugly, plaster Buddha sat in the middle of Thailand's capital city, Bangkok. Visitors put empty soda cans and other trash on it. Then one day a priest decided to take the old statue to his temple. In the moving process it cracked. As the pieces crumbled, the priest noticed something underneath the plaster shell. He gathered some helpers, and they pulled the shell away and inside they found the world's largest chunk of sculptured gold, standing 10 feet high. It had been there for years but no one knew it![47]

Sometimes packaging can be deceptive, can't it? Cereal boxes can make drab cereal look like the most exciting cereal in the world. Billions of dollars is spent on packaging. But sometimes packaging can hide the item (or person) on the inside, as in the case of the Buddha.

I grew up in the area around Phoenix well known for a shopping center called Christown Mall. Christown was named after a farmer whose name was Chris. My friends and I would see Chris on his farm dressed so poorly that you would have thought that he was the poorest man on earth. His house, or should I say shack, was just as shabby looking as Chris.

But it's not wise to judge a book by its cover. Many time people are not as they first appear. Chris, as it turns out, was one of the wisest and wealthiest people in the area. He sold some of his farm land to developers who eventually named a grand shopping center after him. People are more important than their packaging.

Jesus never judged people by their outward appearance. He once saw a scarred and weary woman who had been married five times. He saw beyond her failures and reputation—He saw her heart. He saw a desire to be changed. Jesus revealed the real person she was and gold came forth from an ugly, plaster covering. She went on to fulfill her destiny and redemptive purpose. The whole city benefited from this one golden lady.

Author Mike Murdock writes about what I'm saying this way:

People saw Zaccheus as a conniving, deceptive tax collector. Jesus saw a confused man who longed for a change of heart. The people of Israel saw in Absalom a handsome, articulate leader. He was a traitor and liar. Samson thought Delilah was the most beautiful woman he had ever met. She was a trap who destroyed his championship status.[48]

Get the message?

Sometimes what looks like wealth is false gold. Sometimes hurts, shaping events, and others opinions have covered people of gold with ugly plaster. Remember, the person is the gift, not the package. Real worth must be discerned—go ahead, bring out the best in someone!

• •

**The greatest gift may have to be carefully unwrapped—
revealing the beautiful spirit of a lonely soul.**

56

Trying to Do the Job Alone

The following letter is to an insurance company investigating an accident. The author is unknown but maybe you can relate to what happens when we try to do things on our own.

"I am writing in response to your request for additional information regarding my recent accident. In block number 3 of the accident report form, I put "trying to do the job alone" as the cause of my accident. In your letter you ask that I provide more detailed information, here goes:

"On the date of the accident I was working alone on the roof of a 6-story building. When I completed my roofing work, I discovered that I had about 10 bundles of shingles left over. Rather than carry them down by hand, I decided to lower them on a pallet by using a pulley attached to the side of the building at the 6th floor.

"Securing the rope to my truck bumper, I went up to the roof, swung the pallet out, and loaded the shingles onto it. Then I went back to the ground and untied the rope, holding it tightly to ensure a slow descent of the 720 pounds of shingles. You will note in block number 11 of the accident report form that my weight is 135 pounds.

"Due to my surprise at being jerked off the ground so suddenly, I lost my presence of mind and forgot to let go of the rope. Needless to say, I proceeded up the side of the building at a rapid rate! In the vicinity of the 3rd floor I met the pallet coming down. This explains my fractured skull and broken collarbone.

"At approximately the same time, however, the pallet of shingles struck the ground, spilling over. Devoid of the weight of the shingles, the pallet then weighed about 75 pounds. I again refer you to weight in block number 11.

As you might image, I began a rapid descent down the side of the building.

"In the vicinity of the 3rd floor, I again met the pallet, only this time coming up, which explains my fractured ankle and lacerations of my leg and lower body. On the bright side, striking the pallet that was coming up as I was coming down, did slow my descent enough to lessen my injuries when I landed on the pile of shingles. So fortunately I only cracked three vertebrae and bruised my buttocks.

"As I lay there on top of the shingles in intense pain and unable to stand, I let go of the rope and screamed as I watched the pallet descend down the side of the building and land on me. This explains my strained vocal cords and broken legs.

"I hope this provides you with the information you required as to how the accident happened. I was trying to do the job alone!"[49]

··

There's no reason to go it alone in life—God is always ready, willing, and able to go through life's ups and downs with you!

57

When the Saints Go Marching Out!

A few years ago I presented a series at my church titled, When the Saints Go Marching Out! As the pastor of a large church, I was very concerned that our church had become, well, dare I say it, "churchy." We were really good at doing churchy stuff but had not connected with our community. We were a Christian fellowship—not a church for the community. The series idea focused on how we needed to give our church back to the community. After all, the church is here for the community, not the community for the church.

Most churches are good at being upward in their worship to God and inward in being a church family. We were a great *found* department but a terrible *lost and found* department. It wasn't intentional—we really wanted to help the community. But church culture has a strong magnetic pull inward. It's more of a cultural issue than a desire issue.

A few years ago I wrote a book titled *Church @ Community*, which addresses the issue of giving the church back to the community. The book continues to increase in sales; in fact, we are getting ready for a second printing soon.

Let me share a few one-line ideas that really capture the mission and heart of a church for the community. The church's role in the community is one of contribution, not conquest—liberation, not domination. The church is here to look for a way *in* to the community, not a way *out* of the community. The church is the only organization in the world that exists primarily for its non-members. "Lost" (from a biblical perspective) people matter to God, and therefore should matter to the church. Every sinner has a future, every saint has a past. The church is a community with a cause—the community. Salt can't flavor what it doesn't touch. The church is here to make insider information, outsider information. You come *in* to the presence of God so you can go *out* with the presence of God. The church is here to add value to the community, not take away value.

You can be for God and your community at the same time! That's what Jesus did. He got involved. He left His church in Heaven and went into the community of earth. The Word became flesh and pitched His tent in earth's neighborhood.

Jesus was a neighborhood activist!

That is the way of God. That is the way of Jesus. He saved us—not from a distance, but as a fellow human being. The community needs to see us, the church, as fellow human beings.

....

"Oh when the saints...go marching out...oh when the saints go marching out. Lord I want to be in that number, when the saints go marching out!"

58

Why Go to Church?

A churchgoer wrote a letter to the editor of a newspaper and complained that it made no sense to go to church every Sunday. "I've gone for 30 years now," he wrote, "and in that time I have heard something like 3,000 sermons. But, for the life of me, I can't remember a single one of them. So, I think I'm wasting my time and the pastors are wasting theirs by giving sermons at all."

This started a real controversy in the "Letters to the Editor" column, much to the delight of the editor. Exchanges went on for weeks until someone wrote the following clincher.

"I've been married for 30 years now. In that time my wife has cooked 32,000 meals. But, for the life of me, I cannot recall the entire menu for a single one of those meals. But I do know this, all those meals nourished me and gave me the strength I needed to do my work. If my wife had not given me those meals, I would be physically dead today. Likewise, if I had not gone to church for spiritual nourishment, I would be spiritually dead today!"[50]

Now there's a wise answer! My advice—don't wait for six strong men to take you to church. For many, the only thing worse than going to church is wishing you had!

Church is becoming more relevant and exciting. Many of today's churches are equipping people for life, not just church life. The message is the same but spoken in a contemporary way.

Churches are learning how to speak the language of the community rather than speaking the language of the church.

There is a whole new style of church. Churches are becoming more aware of peoples' needs. Churches are reaching beyond their traditional four walls and connecting with the community.

A few years ago, I was asked how big my church was. I answered, four million! My church is Metro-Phoenix. My church is the community. My congregation numbered 750 but my church was four million. That's true of other pastors too!

I call these types of churches, Tomorrow's Churches Today. Many of us feel more comfortable going to traditional churches. That's OK. But many more Americans need something different—not compromised, but relevant. Churches need to connect the message with the audience. That's what Jesus did and continues to do.

If you aren't going to church, maybe it's time to try church again. Don't neglect the spiritual side of life. Don't neglect the Bible. Your children will benefit, you will benefit, and the community will benefit.

You can choose to be the man who doesn't remember a single sermon and think he's wasting time—or you can choose to be nourished spiritually each week. Which man do you think is more content, more joyful, and more likely to be at peace with God and himself?

••

Why not enjoy a fellowship meal this week, complete with a nice portion of the Word of God and an inspirational dash of prayer!

59

You Might Be a Preacher If...

Bernie and Esther were not the most religious couple. In fact, they really only went to church once a year. As they were leaving the church, the minister said, "Bernie, it sure would be nice to see you and Esther here more than once a year!"

"I know," replied Bernie, "but least we keep the Ten Commandments."

"That's great," the minister said. "I'm glad to hear that you keep the Commandments."

"Yep," says Bernie proudly, "Esther keeps six of them and I keep four."

Welcome to the life of a pastor!

I started my ministry career over 26 years ago. But let me say that being a pastor is a calling first and a career second. You have to be called to go through what most ministers do.

In fact, the calling is stronger than I am.

Most of you will have heard of comedian Jeff Foxworthy's views about, "You Might Be a Red Neck If..." Well, author Stan Toler has written a book called, *You Might Be a Preacher If...*.[51] For many of us he captures the passion of a pastoral calling perfectly. Here are some quotes from his book.

You might be a preacher if you've ever dreamed you were preaching only to awaken and find you were. You might be a preacher if you find yourself counting people at a sporting event. You might be a preacher if you're leading people into the 21st Century and don't know what you are preaching on Sunday. You might be a preacher if you would rather negotiate with a terrorist than the church organist. You might be a preacher if you have ever preached on television but your wife made you get down before you broke something.

You might be a preacher if you have seen it all at weddings. You might be a preacher if you have seen it all at funerals. You might be a preacher if you've ever wanted to start a support group for church janitors. You might be a preacher if you have wanted to give the soundman some feedback of your own. You might be a preacher if you have been asked, "So, what do you do the rest of the week?" You might be a preacher if you've ever been tempted to take an offering at a family reunion. You might be a preacher if you've walked up to the counter at Dairy Queen and ordered a "church split. You might be a preacher if "resisting the devil" and "confronting the church board" are synonymous. You might be a preacher if the words, "And in conclusion," mean absolutely nothing to you."

And finally, "You might be a preacher if you scanned the help-wanted ads on Monday morning!"

Fortunately, the task ahead of us preachers is never as great as the Power behind us. That Power is for you too.

•••

Pastors appreciate your honesty, participation, and sense of humor!

60

The Rodriguez Family Miracle

Miracles happen when giving hearts come together!

That is what we experienced at the Hilton LaPosada Inn in Scottsdale. Let me tell you the story.

At the center of the story is a Native American couple named Kaye and Marcos Rodriguez. Kaye and Marco are the parents of 10 children. One of the children, Kaye's first born, has Down's syndrome. The father of this boy left Kaye when he learned of his son's impairment. Kaye and Marco adopted her brother's three children when her brother unexpectedly died. Add to that Kaye and Marco's own six children and you have quite a family!

Now comes the problem. The Rodriguez family lives in a 700-square-foot home in downtown Phoenix. The children sleep in closets with moldy, leaky ceilings. There is no drywall in the bathroom. The home, while on a big lot, is extremely dilapidated. The children do their homework and eat in the living room on a plastic table. The bathroom has no sink. Marco and Kaye sleep on the sofa. The washer and dryer are kept outside for the lack of space.

Marco works 16 hours a day at Avis Rentals near the airport. Kaye washes, keeps the home going, and makes certain that the children are educated and high achievers. Nine of the children are on the honor role and have received perfect attendance awards. Five of the children play musical instruments. They volunteer with the United Nations for Intertribal Youth.

The solution? The Hilton La Posada heard about the Rodriguez family through their employees. They "adopted" the Rodriguez family as a Christmas giving project. The regional vice president of Hilton Hotels was amazed at the abundance of love and care that Kaye and Marco gave to their children. He noted that the children were thriving without proper living quarters because of the extraordinary positive attitude of their mother and the hard work of their father—

this family wants for nothing, but needs so much.

After the holiday season, the employees wondered if they could build the family a house—their dream house! After meeting with some "see a need—find a solution" community leaders, the miracle started to happen.

These community-minded leaders contacted business, media, local government, educational institutions, and churches. The Larry Elder show picked up the story and the Rodriguez family was featured on the popular, national CBS morning show.

A few months later, we saw the dream of a new house become a reality—a 3,100-square-foot reality. More than 50 businesses donated labor and material to build the Rodriguez home. Even the Marines and Senator John McCain's office was involved.

What a deserving family to be blessed with a home make-over—community style.

••

Miracles happen when giving hearts come together!

61

Trust or Consequences

Trust—that's quite a word. Right now it seems that our whole society is having trouble trusting anyone or anything. We are continually bombarded with leaders in business, government, education, and other sectors of society doing and saying things that violate our trust. Ethical, financial, and moral scandals permeate many levels of our world.

Are we Americans losing our ability to trust? Do things have to go our way for us to trust? Are we doomed to national and local cynicism due to a lack of trust in anything? Is there anyone or anything in which you can place your trust these days? Are we doomed to lives of suspicion and trusting only in ourselves? To trust or not to trust—that is the question.

Like the song says...."I am a rock, I am an island...I touch no one and no one touches me."[52] That's a tough way to live life! It's really more like *existing* than *living*.

I have been concerned about this issue for sometime now. As a pastor, I have noticed that people, whether churched or unchurched, have become more jaded, cynical, and suspicious. Certainly some of this attitude is deserved. We need to use wisdom when deciding in whom and what we trust.

However, I'm concerned with where a lifestyle of *trustlessness* takes us in the long run.

Many people have become like sea urchins in the ocean that have been poked by a stick.

They have closed up. The problem is, when you close up to others, you also close yourself in!

Years ago, as a singles' pastor, I counseled hundred's of newly divorced people. They came into our single's group with vows such as, "I'll never trust a man again." "I'll never trust a woman again." "I'll never fall in love again!" The "I'll nevers" seem comfortable at first but later on can limit one's entire life.

As a response to this issue of distrust, I wrote a book that was published in 2006 titled, *Learning How to Trust Again*. It is important for people to trust—themselves first, then others with discernment. Perhaps with a little wisdom and a lot of sincerity, you will learn to trust again.

....

But as for me, I am like a green olive tree in the house of God; I trust in the lovingkindness of God forever and ever (Psalm 52:8).

62

To Trust or Not to Trust

As we continue on the subject of trust, please be encouraged that you *can* recover your ability to trust. The key is not so much the issue of trust but what we trust in. I believe that it is healthy to trust in someone(s) and something(s). We were designed to trust. To not trust is totally unnatural and severely limits the quality and potential of our lives.

In 1991 during a yearly skiing trip to Taos, New Mexico, I suffered a fall on a double black diamond ski run. I slid out of control at an incredible speed halfway down the mountain. My life was flashing before me.

After what seemed like eons, I finally stopped with a thud on the slope. Celebrating that I was still alive, I did an assessment of my body. I noticed that my left leg was bent at an usual angle—it had hit a tree during the descent. The next few days and weeks were ones of excruciating torture as I waited for medical treatment. I had a compound fracture of my left femur— my thigh bone. The length and severity of the fall had also severely injured the nerves in my leg. Two operations later and sporting a steel rod inserted the entire length of my thigh, I made it back to Phoenix. As I recall, that ski run was called Rattlesnake. I couldn't agree more with the name!

Little did I know that the fun was just beginning. Now I faced physical therapy, and a physical therapist I called "Fang!" My leg (and I) didn't want to cooperate. It was scary to trust someone who was going to cause me more pain. It was easier to trust my leg that begged me for rest. Oh how I wanted

157

to trust that my leg knew what was best. However, I wanted to walk again, maybe even ski again.

I had to make a choice between two painful choices—to trust or not to trust.

It was trust or consequences! I could stay where I was the rest of my life and never regain the full use of my leg—an option my leg voted for. Or I could trust the therapist and be healed. The rest of my body chose that option. Fang won by a close vote!

During the next few months of physical therapy, my leg reminded the rest of my body of how unhappy it was with our decision. However, as the months passed and after much pain, my leg came around to our way of thinking. I stand today with the full use of my leg—and have even skied again.

Get the message? You *can* learn how to trust again. It may be a painful process, but well worth it. Or you can live a very limited life which is not worth it.

．．

Learning to trust again may mean taking small steps at a time—
but take that first step, you'll be glad you did.

63

How We Lose Our Trust

How do we lose our trust?

First of all, Webster's dictionary defines trust as "an assured reliance on the character, ability, strength or trust of someone or something; one in which confidence is placed; a dependence on something future or contingent." In other words, trust is dependent on an object. The object of your trust is what is important. We don't trust in trust, we trust in someone or something. As Christians, we don't trust in trust, we trust in God!

Now what happens if the object we place our trust in fails, disappoints, hurts us, or does not meet our expectations? We act or react—often times more emotionally than rationally. As a result, we make internal vows about what or what not to trust.

In the human reasoning process, individuals evaluate their own experiences, form judgments about those experiences, and then make a vow that will guide future decisions. A vow is defined by Webster's as "…a solemn promise or pledge, esp. one made to God or to a god, dedicating oneself to an act, service or way of life."

For example, when you experience burning your hand on a stove, you most likely will make the following judgments: "that's hot, that hurts, and I don't like it." These judgments lead to a vow, "I'm never going to touch a hot stove again!" This vow then protects you from getting burned in the future… *hopefully!*

Vows vary in intensity from weak to powerful. The more powerful they are, the more the vow influences your decisions and behavior. Here are three rules about vows.

- First, the more traumatic the experience, the more powerful the resulting vow.
- Second, the more often the experience, the more powerful the resulting vow.
- Third, the more recent the experience, the more powerful the resulting vow.

Intensity, frequency, and recency all contribute to the power of the vow.

What does this mean? If something horrible happened to you, more than once, and not too long ago, you will not let yourself get into that situation again in the near future. That can either be good or bad depending on what happened and who or what you trusted!

Many times the vows we make emotionally turn into generalizations such as, "I'm never going to get hurt again." "I'm not going to be betrayed again." "I'm never going to be vulnerable again." Sound familiar? How about other generalizations such as, "All men are…." "All women are…." "All politicians are…." "All liberals are…." "All conservatives are…." "All pastors are…." "All churches are…."

Sound familiar? But there's hope. **We can move from trust *impaired* to trust *repaired* to trust *prepared*.**

....

Vows and judgments and generalizations…oh my!

64

Judgments, Vows, and Generalizations

I'm writing from Pretoria, South Africa. My first trip to South Africa was in the troubled days of 1981. Today the nation has changed so much for the better. It truly is a nation that is learning how to trust again. That doesn't mean that everything here is perfect. However, great steps have been made and are being made for racial reconciliation. The races are working together for a new South Africa, which requires forgiveness from the past and a trust in the future. Frankly, if that can happen in South Africa, it can happen with you and me as well!

Here's a learning-to-trust-again example. Let's consider Bob who has put his pastor on a pedestal. He believes that his pastor can do no wrong, that he always speaks the words of God, that he is a perfect Christian, abounding in wisdom and understanding. But when that pastor, as pastors will, makes a mistake in handling a situation, or says something that touches an exposed nerve in Bob's life, or even falls into a moral problem, then what happens to Bob? He feels hurt or betrayed.

Then Bob may think, *Pastors are all alike. I was stupid to trust Him. If I'm smart, I'll never trust another pastor again.* Did you ever feel that way about a pastor, boss, or public official? I have. I've met many Bobs throughout the years.

Notice how Bob made a judgment and a generalization about all pastors based on one pastor. *Pastors are all alike. I was stupid to trust him.* Then he made a vow, *I'll never trust another pastor again.* He judged, generalized, and made a vow.

Judgments and vows are not all bad. If you touch your hand on a hot stove burner and decide not to do that again, that is wisdom. However, if you decided never to touch a stove again, that would be overgeneralizing. Many times when you generalize, you live by general lies.

What about Bob? Perhaps he should have been more realistic about his pastor. Perhaps making his pastor and church a god created an expectation in Bob that only God could fulfill. Perhaps Bob should get involved in a church again, only this time he needs to focus more on Jesus.

When I broke my leg skiing, I had to put things in perspective. *Maybe all ski runs are not evil! Perhaps I should ski again but this time not on double black diamond runs. That's wisdom, not over reaction.*

....

"We should be careful to get out of an experience only the wisdom that is in it—and stop there; lest we be like the cat that sits down on a hot stove-lid. She will never sit down on a hot stove-lid again and that is well; but she will never sit down on a cold one any more."

—Mark Twain

65

Regaining Your Ability to Trust

Thank you for walking with me on this journey through the issue of trust. Again I'm writing this from Pretoria, South Africa—truly a nation learning to trust again.

The following are some very practical steps you can take to regain your ability to trust. It will be hard work, and you will need wisdom to succeed, but well worth the effort. You may have to give up to go up.

First, let's recognize and stop using extreme and reactionary vows and ways of coping that have trapped us. Vows such as, "I'll never trust a man or woman again, I'm not going to be hurt again, I won't be vulnerable again, all pastors are…," end up trapping us and limiting our potential. These thoughts trap us in, more than keep others out.

Next, let's leave old ways behind and free ourselves for new directions—in other words, repent. You enter your next phase clean when you get rid of the old emotional baggage that weighs you down. Repenting reactions such as hate, resentment, vengeance, and cynicism means asking God for forgiveness from those shaping events, people, or institutions that have hurt you. When you forgive others, you free yourself.

Next, let's be realistic about what and in whom we place our trust next time. We must use wisdom. Perhaps you should not date someone with a history of broken relationships and a pattern of infidelity if you want a long-term relationship. That's not judging, that is using wisdom. Perhaps you should not invest in a company that has no long-term credibility. Again, that's using wisdom. Perhaps you shouldn't ski the double black diamond run because you have too much trust in your own ability!

Learn to use wisdom before making choices, and trusting will become much easier.

Finally, please persevere. It takes time to get over long-time habits and ways of thinking. If your ability to trust has been torn apart, know that it can be mended—one wise choice at a time.

••

God's power frees you from the past. He also gives you wisdom for the future when you learn to trust Him totally.

66

Just Because

Last year my wife, Becky, came up with an idea that was a blessing to the community and to our church. We all are familiar with the lines at some of the huge department and electronic stores in the wee early hours the day after Thanksgiving. Well, Becky suggested we serve free coffee and hot chocolate to the freezing shoppers—just because! No agenda, nothing to be gained for our church or cause—just because we want to serve and bless people.

She called the local Best Buy store, and received permission from the manager to serve the morning holiday cheer. We got up at 3 o'clock in the morning, and drove to the nearby coffee store. They had been working on coffee and hot chocolate for us all night. After loading the truck with six huge urns of liquid warmth, off we went to serve the 600+ people waiting in line at about 5 in the morning. Now that's commitment! We are talking motivated shoppers!

As you can imagine, we we're greeted with great joy! I felt like quoting the verse in the Bible, "…behold, I bring you good news of great joy which shall be for all the people…." Coffee and hot chocolate for all! After serving warm coffee to the cold community of shoppers for a few hours, the only thing that could have made the morning better was a Port-A-Jon! Many times when you meet one need, you create another. Live and learn!

Here's the point. Becky wanted to help others—just because! Service without an agenda. The hot beverages were not a means to an end but the end itself.

Meet the need, not our agenda—just because.

Wouldn't it wonderful if we had a little more of that attitude? In today's world, it seems like everything we do is motivated by a hidden agenda. We use our positions, our jobs, our friends, and our community to advance our philosophy, politics, or cause. It has become more about conquest than contribution. Have we lost our just because? Are we beginning to politicize everything? Does there have to be something in it for me to do anything at all?

The truth is, the more you push your agenda, the less likely it is that you will accomplish your agenda. Jesus came not to be served but to serve (see Matt. 20:28). That is what made Jesus so unusual. People were the end, not a means to an end. Jesus met their needs—just because. It wasn't political, it was humanitarian.

Jesus was into transformations, not transactions. Transformations come when you give your life, no strings attached, to serving, not getting—just because!

....

Just because...try it!

67

Social Entrepreneurialism

In my book titled *Church @ Community*, I explore one of the most misunderstood verses in the Bible. This verse, if understood and applied, has incredible potential to create a win/win for both the church and the community. It's about social entrepreneurialism and the church was given instructions by Jesus to embrace it.

Let's explore the verse: "Let your light shine before men *in such a way* that they may see your good works, and glorify your Father who is in heaven" (Matt. 5:16). Jesus talks about works *in such a way* that catch the heart of the community and open eyes to the reality of Christ's desire to make the entire world better, not just the church. These works redefine God, church, and Christians in the eyes of the community. Their response is worship,

"Wow—if this is what the church does, I'm interested!"

Jesus wants us to look for a way *into* the community, not a way out. Works create a church-community connection that brings awareness of Christ through the church to the community. These works are real, tangible, and lasting—something the community can relate to. Works are the Word becoming flesh and dwelling within the community.

There are many works that the church can do that are helpful. But there are works *in such a way* that really catch the heart of the community.

A few years ago I was in Mombasa, Kenya, located in the east-central region of Africa, to speak in the largest church in the country. The pastor showed me pictures of himself and his 20,000-member congregation cleaning up trash along four miles of the main highway between the cities of Nairobi and Mombasa. In fact, he was on the front page of every major newspaper in Kenya. Why? His church was doing something about a major problem that everyone was aware of—trash! The church moved from talking to doing.

The community response was overwhelming! The national press picked up the story. Even the president of Kenya at that time, President Moi, spoke about the church's laudable community contribution and that there was something spiritual about what the church had done.

Although there were many things churches could do in Kenya, this was a good work *in such a way* that addressed, in a real and tangible way, a major need. That's social entrepreneurialism that creates spiritual awareness.

Want to know what those good works *in such a way* are in your community? Go ask the police, social services, or city council. They will tell you! Remember, people have bodies, minds, and souls, and we are shortchanging them if we don't try to meet the needs of all three.

···

**Commit to becoming a social entrepreneur in your neighborhood—
you won't regret the decision.**

68

Recapturing Volunteerism

A mother was preparing breakfast for her sons, Kevin, age 5, and Ryan, age 3. The boys began to argue over who would get the first pancake. Their mother saw an opportunity for a moral lesson.

"If Jesus was sitting here, He would say, 'Let my brother have the first pancake, I can wait.'"

Kevin turned to his younger brother and said, "Ryan, you be Jesus!"

Sound familiar? I've been through a few of those discussions when my sons, Matthew and Jonathan, were younger. On second thought, I'm still going through them!

Unfortunately, volunteering has become a lost value in today's culture. Do you realize Jesus *volunteered* to leave His world to come to ours? He was safe and sound in Heaven. Everything was perfect! However, there was a need in our neighborhood and He volunteered to meet it. He left the comfort of His church. He got out of the seat and onto the street. He didn't serve them because they were saved, He served them because *He* was saved. He found a need and met it!

We read in the Bible that during a very tough time for Israel, God was looking for a volunteer. A king had just died, and someone needed to speak for God to the nation. The Lord asks, "whom shall I send, and who will go...?" Isaiah's response,

"Here am I, send me!"

(See Isaiah 6:7-9.) He got out of the seat and onto the street.

There are many needs and opportunities for service in your neighborhood. We are here because our community is here. In today's society, many have become disconnected from their community. We expect business or government to do everything for us. Frankly, the government shouldn't have to do everything. Have we come so far that community service is considered punishment? The truth is you and I can more quickly improve our communities than the government can. I always say, "If it's going to be, it starts with me!" Whatever you can tolerate, you can't change.

Shirley Chisholm once said that service is the rent that you pay for room on this earth. The community needs you to be all that it can be. To church people I say, get involved in the community—not just the church. Hospitals, libraries, community action programs, food banks, and even airports are looking for volunteers. One night or a few hours a week is a small price to pay for a great community.

· ·

"We make a living by what we get, but we make a life by what we give."

—Winston Churchill

69

Here Come the Judges

Let's face it, some people find fault like there's a reward for it! My advice, be a good-finder, not an habitual fault-finder.

Take Mildred, for example. You may know a Mildred. Mildreds are everywhere—not just in church. They are busy in business, mainline media, schools, neighborhoods, everywhere there are people, there are Mildreds!

Mildred, the church gossip and self-appointed monitor of the church's morals, kept sticking her nose into other people's business. Several members did not approve of her extra-curricular activities, but feared her enough to maintain their silence. She made a mistake, however, when she accused George, a new member, of being an alcoholic after she saw his old pickup parked in front of the town's only bar one afternoon. She emphatically told George and several others that everyone knew what he was doing in the bar.

George, a man of few words, stared at her for a moment, then turned and walked away. He didn't explain, defend, or deny. He said nothing. Later that evening, George drove to Mildred's house and parked his pickup in front of Mildred's house—and left it there all night.[53]

Enough said! Good story, huh?

Those who continually judge end up being judged themselves.

"For whatever measure you deal out to others, it will be dealt to you in return" (Luke 6:38). That principle works both positively and negatively.

You sow it, you reap it! In fact, the Bible says in Hosea, "sow a wind, reap a whirlwind!" It comes back to you even worse. Just ask Mildred.

Why do we like to judge? First of all, we like to be right. It makes us feel in control. It serves our desire for significance. It justifies our position. It's a means to an ego-driven end. While the above reasons are not true for all people, they certainly are for many.

Let me tell you two secrets to getting along with others. If you're going to judge, first judge yourself. Jesus told a group of people who loved to judge to examine themselves first. "And why do you look at the speck in your brother's eye, but do not notice the log that is in your own eye" (Matt. 7:3). Don't you wish everyone examined themselves first before judging others? After all, logs are bigger than specks!

Second, the Bible says judging should be for building others up rather than tearing them down. Judging for the sake of judging or destructive judging for advancing your own agenda is not productive. Be constructive, not destructive!

If the boat has a hole in it, don't stand on the shore yelling at the hole, jump in the water and go help fix the boat. Don't micromanage the hole—fix it. Be a part of the solution, don't add to the problem! Speak the truth in love, not with a glove or a shove!

That's true for our friends, communities, nation, places of employment, churches, all of the places where we touch others' lives. Look for a way in, not a way out!

....

Don't be a Mildred.

70

Good News!

Here we go again. It's that time of the year. Say good-bye to the old and hello to the new. I don't know about you but I love new starts. I want to learn from the past, enjoy and live the present, and look forward to the adventure of the future. I like the concept of *new*.

Did you know the Bible has heaps to say about the concept of *new*? There's a *New* Testament, a *new* life, a *new* covenant, a *new* commandment to love one another, and a *new* name. When we receive Christ as Savior we become a *new* creation, all things are *new*. God's mercies are *new* every morning, not the same old same old! We sing a *new* song and have a *new* self because *new* things have come. One day there will be a *new* Heaven, *new* earth, and a *new* Jerusalem.

Folks, that's what I call *the good news!* The angel at Christ's birth had it right,

"behold, I bring you good *news* of great joy...."

That angel, in my opinion, was talking about two kinds of news—news and new*s*. That's what I love about the New Year, it can be a new start. The closing of a chapter, the opening of a new. Going from the old to the new, wiser and stronger. Running the race looking ahead, not behind. Ever run a race looking backward? It's not easy. It takes three times the effort and gets you nowhere!

Two grown men were being interviewed because their parents were alcoholics and they had grown up to lead very different lives. One son was an alcoholic, worse than his parents. His life was in shambles. The other son was a model citizen, a nondrinker, and a respected businessman. In the interview, both men were asked the same question. "How did you end up the way you are in life?"

The amazing thing was that both of the sons had the same answer to the question. "With my background, what would you expect?" One learned from his experience and the other one couldn't move past it. One closed the chapter on the old and started a new chapter, the other one didn't. One learned how to run the race looking forward. The other, whether intentionally or unintentionally, looked backward.

We should not ignore the past, and chemical imbalances may contribute to behavior, but the past doesn't have to rule our lives. Let's learn from the past and go boldly into the present and future! God wants you to get your direction from Him, not the past.

Each new year affords us an opportunity to start with *good news, not bad news—new news, not old news!* It will take God's help, making some right choices, forgiveness, humility, turning your head and closing some chapter's. But that is what New Year's has the potential to be about. Happy News Year!

• •

There's no future living in the past. Focus on good news!

71

Go Easy on the Oats and Brandy

That's quite a title, isn't it?

At 4:10 A.M. on April 29, 1903, 70-80 million tons of rock slid off the face of Turtle Mountain killing approximately 75 people and trapping many in the little town of Frank, Alberta, Canada. Among those trapped by the slide were 17 miners who took 12 hours to dig out of their entombment. The elation of reaching daylight was short lived as their eyes adjusted and the panorama of their devastated town came into focus. These men were the last of the survivors to be found—that is until Charlie was discovered.

About a month after that fateful day, and at the end of efforts to reopen the main entrance to the Frank mine, Charlie the mine horse was found alive. Dwelling in complete darkness, he had endured by drinking seepage water, eating the bark off of mine timbers, and breathing air from the vertical escape shaft the 17 trapped miners had dug to escape that first day. If horses can experience elation, Charlie must have experienced it then—that is until he died the same day from an overdose of oats and brandy given to him by his rescuers. What testing could not take, celebration robbed from Charlie. Pastor Tim Davis passed along this story to me. It's a good one, isn't it?

Sadly, Charlie's end is not unlike the experience of many who have survived an episode of testing or darkness in their lives. They were down to nothing in their finances. Their marriage was on the rocks. Their business was on the verge of bankruptcy. Their child had run away from home. They experienced a loss of someone very dear. You have probably had a similar dwelling-in-the-dark Charlie experience. I know I have.

Have you noticed that during those Charlie times your prayer life improves dramatically? You become spiritual because there is nowhere else to turn. I've always said that nothing improves your prayer life like a real good reason for praying. When many are in the middle of Charlie-type trials, their declarations rise to God.

"God, I'll do anything...just rescue me!

If you will get me out of this mess, I will serve you the rest of my life! If you rescue me, why I'll even go to church!" Sound familiar?

Then all of a sudden, rescue comes. Somehow everything works out. Along came a new customer with a big order, a clean bill of health after a last-chance treatment, or a point of contention in a tenuous relationship is resolved. Coincidence, or has God chosen to remain anonymous?

Many times, the real test is immediately after the Charlie times are over. When everything is good again, have we learned from the experience? Or do we allow others to drown out the lesson with good intentions?

••

**When darkness ends and God's deliverance arrives,
go easy on the oats and brandy!**

72

Military 101

Hope is not a strategy!

M any people I meet expect to achieve their goals and desires magically. They hope to accomplish their goals by winning some kind of lottery that gives them what they want without thinking or working.

Very few win a lottery—they are extreme exceptions. If you want to live by betting on being an exception, you will most probably be very disappointed most of the time. May I suggest a better way of achieving your goals or desires? Develop a strategy. God will help you every step of the way.

My friend Grady Daniels, a retired military man, wrote a short description on objectives and strategies that he calls Military 101. We can all benefit from what Grady shares:

Objective (At the highest levels, this is sometimes called Grand Strategy): What is it that you ultimately want? Your answer is your *objective*.

Strategy is the art of deciding the big-picture way of obtaining your objective.

Operational Art is choosing and organizing your campaigns so that they make sense and work together toward obtaining the objective and in support of your strategy.

A Campaign is a series of battles aimed at a specific part of achieving the objective.

Tactics is the art of winning a battle.

A Battle is simply the fight you are engaged in at the moment.

Now, let's bring Military 101 into everyday life.

Objective: Happy wife.

Strategy: Show your wife a wonderful time on your anniversary.

Operational Art: Identify a good jeweler that has the bracelet you know she wants. Find a good florist in the neighborhood. Remember the name of that posh restaurant your wife has always wanted to go to (if you can't remember, ask your kids).

Campaign: Go to the jeweler, buy the bracelet, pick up roses on the way home, take her to dinner. In that order. (Going to the jeweler at 11 P.M. after dinner won't work, and she won't be happy.)

Tactics: Be sure the car has gas. Have a clean suit ready. Leave early, don't be late. Avoid the accident at the next intersection. Know what time the jeweler closes. Ditto the florist. Buy roses (get more than one). Brush teeth. Be charming, etc.

Battle: Put all of your tactics to work to win all the little battles on the way toward achieving your objective.

At the end of your anniversary evening—Voilá! A happy wife!

Military 101 works in the workplace, church, in the community, and in most situations. Plan ahead and achieve your goals.

••

Hope is not a strategy.

73

Doberman Pinscher Strategy

Here's a concept. Let's say someone has two Doberman pinschers guard-ing his house from robbers. If you are the robber, all you have to do is throw a piece of steak into the yard, let the Dobermans fight over it, and then go right into the house and rob it. (Of course, you better have another steak ready for them to fight over so you can get back out of the house!) The core instinct of most Doberman pinschers is that eating the steak takes precedent over guarding the house.

That's quite an interesting way or strategy of robbing a guarded house, isn't it? OK, I know there are some dog trainers out there who are not agree-ing with me, but you get the idea. We people fall victim to the Doberman pinscher strategy quite frequently. We need to keep our focus on the main objective.

For instance, consider this Bible example. The apostle Paul was in a very difficult situation. He was on trial for his faith before the leaders of his faith. The accusers were two groups of religious people—the Sadducees and Pharisees. Each of these groups was trying to accuse Paul of wrongdoing. But while they were on the same team, so to speak, they each held differing the-ological views. One group believed in the resurrection of Jesus Christ and the other group did not.

How did Paul get out of this situation? He says in Acts 23:6, "I am a Pharisee, a son of Pharisees; I am on trial for the hope and resurrection of the dead!" He threw the "steak" of theological differences into the religious council's yard—which meant trouble in River City! What was the result? The Pharisees and Sadducees started arguing with each other. The Bible describes the scene as a "great dissension," "divided," "great uproar," "argue heatedly," and "afraid Paul might be torn to pieces." It was a dog fight. Incidentally, after that scene Paul walked away with a life insurance policy and an all expense paid trip by the Romans to Rome for fear of his safety. Why? He knew about the Doberman pinscher strategy.

We can apply this to our lives, community, and country. Many times we allow little steaks of individual differences to divide us. Take a married couple who has a long history of unresolved differences. All it takes is for someone or something to throw a steak at them to spark an argument and they forget about focusing on their marriage vows.

Winning the argument, staying in power, and proving your point becomes a more important steak than the relationship, the vision, or the mission. This is the situation throughout many countries, communities, and businesses today.

Let's be wise and understanding, and learn that winning the argument is not more important than losing the nation, community, or relationship.

Let's major on the majors.

Let's not fall victim to impulses, winning the battle but losing the war.

•••

Enjoy the steak, but don't loose sight of the main objective!

74

Mission Possible

I offer three suggestions about how to stay out of dog fights in relationships both personal and in the marketplace. When best friends, customers, or allies turn on one another, "Houston, we have a problem!"

Preventable broken relationships cause more emotional baggage than anything else in life.

Suggestion 1. Remember the mission.

What was the dogs' mistake? They forgot their main objective. Their mission was to guard the house. Adam and Eve forgot too. They were too busy eating apples (the early form of steak) to guard the Garden from intruders. That is easy to do. Remember, preserving and maintaining your marriage and relationships are more important than losing your future, children, or emotional health (assuming the relationships are not abusive). Winning the battle is not worth losing the war. Remember the big picture!

Suggestion 2. Discover preventative maintenance.

The best solution to preserving healthy relationships is to keep unresolved issues from piling up. The Bible says, "Do not let the sun go down on your anger" (Eph. 4:26). That is great advice. Little things that pile up become big things—real big things! Do not let issues get to the point where one party has checked out, and has decided it's not worth the effort. It takes two to negotiate. You can not negotiate with a terrorist or a checked-out wounded person or customer.

Suggestion 3. Dare to negotiate.

The Dobermans could have guarded the house *and* could have eaten the steak by guarding the house first, scaring off the robber, and then enjoying the fruit of their labors. Mission first, steak second, and above all, keep the relationship secure and intact. The only downside is that you have to share. We don't always like that!

Relationships, whether in the home, the business world, the church family, or in the community, can be fragile. There are numerous stories in the Bible when personalities clash, misunderstandings occur, and tempers cause pain. Take time to read the Bible as a real-life guide to handling relationships. The problems people had in biblical times are no different from the ones we encounter today when dealing with others.

••

**There is wise advice and guidance in God's love letter to you—
read it today for nourishment and refreshment.**

75

Fear, Anger, or Love?

Here's my advice about learning how to avoid falling into the Doberman steak trap. Assuming that both parties are willing to work at the relationship, dare to negotiate, communicate, and move forward together toward a resolution.

There are three basic emotions in human beings—fear, anger, and love. Fear is moving away. Anger is moving against. Love is moving toward. Many times in conflict one or both parties either shut up or shut down. That is called fear. Hopelessness sets in, and it is feared that the issue will never change or be resolved.

Other times, one or both parties attack each other. That's anger. We tend to hide (fear) or hurl (anger) just like Adam and Eve in the Garden. Reacting with anger seldom brings resolution.

Negotiation and resolution require the greatest emotion of all—love.

Actually love is more than emotion—it's intelligent emotion. It comes from God. Love is moving toward the other person or issue for resolution. It's proactive. It's courageous! Love dares to say, "I feel…I think…I would like…." Love accepts responsibility for past mistakes. Love takes the higher road of solving problems, not personalizing problems.

Love requires maturity. It's much better to be a 35-year-old person than a 7-year-old person five times. Love is moving toward each other. Love brings both parties to the table again. Each has the freedom and the responsibility to say, "This is what I think when…this is how I feel when…this is what I would like in order to stop thinking and feeling this way."

Negotiation means that you may not get everything you want. However, you get *some* things that you want, and maybe just what you *need*. Negotiation requires communication. You have moved forward. Perhaps you have even acknowledged the other person's point of view. Perhaps you may even give up a little to gain a lot. Remember the Dobermans? Save the relationship and share the steak! Forgiveness makes the future possible.

Christ came to bring God and humans back to the table so their broken relationship would be restored. The restoration of relationships—from bad to good, good to better, better to great—is why Jesus came to earth. He is the Ultimate Marriage Counselor, Conflict Manager, Bridge Builder, and Third-Party Negotiator.

Love caused God to reach out to us. Love can cause us to mend relationships and embrace an enjoyable future.

....

Choose love!

76

The Tanzanian Angel

The Tanzanian angel. I know what you're thinking. Doesn't he mean the Tasmanian devil? Let me explain.

I was invited to speak at a Bible school located in Arusha, Tanzania, in sub-Saharan Africa. Arusha is located near Mount Kilimanjaro, "Kili" as the locals call it. The school is called The Joshua Foundation and is run by Dr. Alan Stephenson, a missionary of New Zealand descent who was born in Tanzania. His grandparents came as missionaries from New Zealand and America to Tanzania. Little did they know the legacy they would leave in this most beautiful of African nations.

Alan Stephenson's father, John Griffith Stephenson, was raised in this untamed, wilderness part of the world. He was blessed with great pioneering abilities. His knowledge of the country, peoples, ethics, and languages made him a true son of present-day Tanzania. His involvement in World War II in an African context, plus experiencing the colonial days thereafter, persuaded him that there had to be a better way than mere foreign policy to develop a nation.

In 1961 came the new independent government in Tanzania. This is when Alan's father's real macro-missionary work began. Nyerere, the country's founding father and a good friend of Alan's father, asked him to assume the role of National Parks Director for Tanzania. This was a huge assignment encompassing vast areas of the country that were swarming with wildlife. The need was immense for a planned, intelligent, integrated approach to the country's commercial development, as well as conserving and protecting the large animal population.

Steve, as most called Alan's father, was a primary mover in establishing the fabulous Ngorongoro Crater and the Highlands as conservation areas. Here the Maasai tribal people could continue grazing their cattle in unison with the increasing number of tourists visiting the vast and interesting land.

Steve established Gombe National Park where Jane Goodall worked. He also opened Mikumi National Elephant Park, where he lived for many years. He surveyed the vast Ruaha area which was set aside as a national park. His work in Tanzania as National Parks Director developed an infrastructure and policy for parks in Africa.

Wildlife tourism is Tanzania's greatest source of foreign income, and the national park system is one of the best in Africa. I've heard it said that Dr. David Livingstone, one of Africa's still revered, true heroes, called country development the three inseparable C's—Christianity, commerce, and civilization.

Steve Stephenson and his Christian roots helped develop an entire nation. As the Bible says, Jesus is the Savior of *all*.

Everybody benefits from Christ whether they accept Him or not.

Everyone who lives in Tanzania, and others throughout the world have benefited from Steve's work. This is not transformation—is TransForNation!

The next time you see one of those National Geographic Africa documentaries, you have also benefited from the Tanzanian Angel!

· ·

Accept the opportunities that God presents to you through others— you may be surprised at the transformation!

77

Changing *Their* World

I recently heard a phrase that really caught my attention—we can't change *the* world, but we can change *their* world. The phrase was used in the context of supporting an orphanage in Romania.

In other words, we can't do everything, but we can do one thing, something, somewhere, to change *their* world! Think about it, if everyone did something, all those somethings would add up to changing the world. We change the world by changing their world.

Changing their world begins with changing our world—changing the way we see things. It starts with looking past everyone else's faults. It starts with seeing the big picture, and by moving from a reactive to proactive attitude. It starts by putting down our agenda so we can serve the community or others for their sake, not ours. Until somebody does something, nobody does anything.

I was inspired by the 80-year-old couple who have served in a local senior center in our community for many years. They wake up early in the morning, make the coffee and cook for people in need. This is their ministry. They haven't changed *the* world, but they have changed *their* world. President George W. Bush publicly acknowledged and honored this couple for their unselfish acts of kindness.

What can you and I do to change *their* world?

Some suggestions: write a card to someone you know is going through a tough time. Volunteer at a hospital or community agency. Share Christ in word or deed with someone looking for answers. Commit to being more others-centered rather than self-centered. Be more agreeable at home. Help orphans in Romania or your own neighborhood. You know you see others in need every day.

Jesus changed *their* world. Whether a prostitute, a crowd of 5,000, a blind man, or a rich person. He changed their world! With Christ in you, you can too! Jesus also changed the world by dying on the Cross to redeem humanity from sin. He came from Heaven to earth to *show* the way, not teach or preach the way.

It's time to give the church back to the community. It's time to get out of the seat and into the street. God designed the church to be a community *for* the community.

....

We can't change *the* world, but we can change *their* world!

78

Back to Your Future

When you are in your 50s like I am, you begin to realize that the future is *now*. The only thing worse than planning for the future is wishing you had! It takes time, effort, and making some really tough decisions that could affect you for the rest of your life. Just ask the multitudes who haven't planned their future and now wish they had! Learn from other people's mistakes.

Here's a story about a man planning for his future.

Dear Spike,

I have been unable to sleep since I forced my daughter to break off her engagement to you. Will you forgive and forget? I was much too sensitive about your mohawk, tattoo, and pierced nose. I now realize motorcycles aren't really that dangerous, and I really should not have reacted the way I did to the fact that you have never held a job. I am sure, too, that some other very nice people live under the bridge in the park.

Sure my daughter is only 17 and wants to marry you instead of going to Harvard on a full scholarship, but after all, you can't learn everything about life from books. I sometimes forget how backward I can be. I was wrong. I was a fool. I have now come to my senses, and you have my blessing to marry my daughter.

Sincerely,

Your future father-in-law

P.S. Congratulations on winning the Powerball jackpot lottery![54]

Oh, the creativity of some people! Now there's an example of planning for your future! However, even if you win the rat race, you're still a rat!

While I don't condone the future father-in-law's motives, I do appreciate his awareness in planning for the future. The Bible says in Proverbs 13:22, "A good man leaves an inheritance to his children's children." That's planning for three generations.

Do you realize that there are many different types of inheritances that you can plan for right now? There are financial inheritances. There are family inheritances or heirlooms. There are spiritual inheritances. There are memory inheritances. You don't have to be rich to leave an inheritance. You just need to start planning.

The future is now.

Why not begin this week to plan for your spiritual future? If you don't go to church, give church a chance. If you have never considered the Bible, give it a chance. If you're not into the churchy stuff, read Proverbs. There's some great wisdom in there. Then read about Jesus in the Gospels. There's gold in "that thar" Book!

Take advantage of the time you have to plan for your spiritual future. Who knows? You just might leave an inheritance that continues for generations! You can live way beyond your earthly life through a positive, redemptive legacy.

• •

The time is *now* for a future *later*.

79

Seasons in Life

Do you know there are two major seasons in our lives? The Bible calls these seasons strength and wisdom. There is a time for strength. Then as you gain experience and lose some strength, the season changes to wisdom (hopefully)! Interested? I thought you would be.

Proverbs 20:29 reveals to us this truth, "The glory of young men is their strength, and the honor of old men is their gray hair." Gray hair is an Old Testament symbol of wisdom. So there is a strength time and a wisdom time in our lives.

I loved the strength time in my life. I could stay out all night drag racing up and down Central Avenue in Phoenix. I could get in at 4:30 A.M. and get up at 6:30 A.M. and work all day. I could play two rounds of golf in a row in the summer. I could eat eggs, bacon, and the eight food groups, stuffed with cholesterol! I remember water skiing for hours at a time. One time when I was a young business owner I stayed awake for three days in a row to get out a rush job. In those days, what I lacked in wisdom I could make up for in strength. If I tried that now, I would be toast! Know what I mean?

Today, I eat things like bran flakes, read the newspaper, drink coffee, and have air-conditioning in my car. In my youth, air-conditioning was just something that robbed horsepower. Today I wouldn't leave home without it! The hair that was on my head is growing out my nose and ears. I'm not losing hair, I'm gaining head! It takes me three Snickers bars to get around the golf course while my young friends watch in wonder. I even listen to classical music! Why I'm even starting to look like my father. Oh, the cost of wisdom.

You might say I've transitioned, morphed, or maybe I'm just a little older, and hopefully wiser. I'm in my 50s and in the wisdom time of life. Sometimes confusion about which time of life we are in causes identity problems and mid-life crises.

Both of these seasons are good and God.

That's the way He designed life. Wisdom people, remember that the younger people are in the strength time of their lives. Their music will be louder, they will drive somewhat faster—they are in that season of life. To the strength people, remember that the wisdom of others could save your life. Wisdom is needed for you to be all that you can be.

Generations working together—both strength and wisdom—are what make communities complete.

··

Wisdom and strength were meant to *complete* one another, not *compete* with one another.

80

Thinking—On Purpose

People worldwide are having an epiphany on the subject of purpose. Pastor Rick Warren's book, *The Purpose Driven Life*, has sold over 25 million copies. It was reported that a woman held captive by an escaped convict quoted and read parts of Warren's book to him that apparently changed his perspective on life—and may have saved her life!

The inventor of the microphone had purpose in mind when he invented the microphone. He wanted to capture sound and magnify it for an audience to hear. Purpose is an intent, a reason. The microphone is the *way* it is because of *why* it is.

Purpose is what was in the mind of the Creator when He created all things. God is a God of purpose. "The Lord made everything for its own purpose..." (Prov. 16:4). Do you realize the Creator had a purpose in mind for you and me when He created us? You are the *way* you are because of *why* you are!

When the Lord made you, He looked at you and said, "I'll never do that again"! I mean that in a positive and unique way. The fact that you are here means that this generation needs something that only you can offer. Could it be that God has been preparing you for His destiny designed especially for you?

The Bible says, "For David, *after he had served the purpose of God in his own generation*, fell asleep, and was laid among his fathers..." (Acts 13:36). David fulfilled his purpose and the purposes of God in his own generation, then he died. Just like David, you and I have a very special purpose in *this* life for our *own* generation.

I've seen people changed by activating their purpose. I've seen Generation X turn to Generation NEXT after discovering their purpose.

Perhaps the convict who held the woman hostage ended up escaping from a bigger jail—the jail of ignorance of purpose. Ignorance of purpose does not cancel purpose. It just makes you miserable until you discover it.

Sometimes great problems in communities are caused by great people not knowing their purpose in life.

If you don't know what your purpose in life is, your priority is clear—figure it out!

....

Ask God to reveal His purpose for your life—then go for it!

81

Investing Time—On Purpose

If you don't know what your purpose in life is, ask God to reveal it to you.

Your priorities flow out of your purpose.

Your purpose determines what is important in your life. Jesus was aware of His purpose, so decisions were easy for Him. Because He knew where He was going, He got there. Jesus was purpose-driven. He knew He had come "to seek and save." He knew His assignment in life was to do the will of His Father God. The Bible says, "The Son of God appeared for this purpose, to destroy the works of the devil" (1 John 3:8). Purpose is the design of God in your life. You are more productive, prosperous, and peaceful when living in your purpose.

Peter Lowe has written about two types of people. He calls them *directional thinkers* and *limitational thinkers*. Limitational thinkers are too occupied with traveling to give much thought to their destination. They don't plan their lives. Their lives evolve as they go along. Their friends are mostly chosen by proximity. Their work is mostly chosen by what is conveniently available. Whatever happens, happens.

Directional thinkers plan their lives. During high school they are choosing their college. During college they are planning their careers. During their career years, they are working toward predetermined positional advancement. When they retire, naturally, they are prepared. They sense a purpose for their existence, and they can usually tell you what that purpose is. They invest their time in the priorities of life.[55]

They are purpose-driven but not purpose over-driven.

Limitational thinkers *spend* time. Directional thinkers *invest or plan* their time. There is a huge difference between the two—the results at the end of life prove it. In other words, success in all areas of life is by choice, not by chance, for most people.

Are you a limitational thinker or a directional thinker? I started out a limitational thinker. Now I'm a directional thinker. I choose investing over spending. The results, rewards, and relationships are so much better. The great British prime minister Benjamin Disraeli said, "The secret of success is constancy of purpose."

···

Purpose is one of the *ways* of God.

82

Moving From Dream to Done

A few years ago I was in Nakuru, Kenya, speaking at a large church. In fact, it was right before the summer Olympic games in Sydney, Australia. This was my eighth time to Kenya. I love Kenya and the Kenyans. Kenyans are so full of life and vision. They believe it and talk it, but there's just one problem. They never seem to get to their vision.

Of course this is not only a Kenyan problem. Many people are dreamers but not doners. They have a hard time moving from dream to done, from revelation to reality, from invisible to visible, and from alpha to omega.

Realizing that the Kenyans national source of pride is winning the marathon in the Olympics, I thought I would try and make a point with my Kenyan friends. As I stood in front of more than a thousand Kenyans at a church service I asked them, "How many Kenyans here have a vision of winning the Olympic gold medal for the marathon event?" Without one bit of hesitation the crowd stood up and cheered. They all had a vision! Then I asked, "How many here believe that Kenyans have it in their DNA to win the Olympic gold medal for the marathon event?" We had revival! Everyone was in agreement.

"Now, if that Kenyan has a vision to win the Olympics, and has it in his DNA to win the Olympic gold medal BUT he never practices—will he win the gold medal?"

There was silence. There was no more revival. I thought I was in trouble.

Here's a lesson we all need to learn. You can have a great vision, you can even have it in your DNA to succeed, but if you don't have the right values, your vision will seldom become a reality. In the case of the Kenyans, they all had a great vision, they certainly have it in their DNA, but their lack of commitment disables their vision every time.

Now let's apply this lesson to our lives.

Values can either make you or break you.

The truth is many of us want to be successful but lack the values required to get us there. Values are important. Values drive your behavior. Vision is the thermostat but values run the heating and air conditioning unit.

How do you turn unfulfilled potential into fulfilled reality? By embracing enabling values that can get you to your vision! You move from tell-a-vision to do-a-vision! That's the way God designed it. Every person can greatly enhance their chances of winning the Olympics by adopting the value of self-discipline.

· ·

A vision unmanaged leads to frustration!

83

Putting Out Fires

Every one wants unity but how do you achieve unity? That's a good question, isn't it? How can you achieve unity in your family, between cities and nations, in your business, with your spouse, or in your church? While we all talk unity, many times on the way to unity things end up worse than they started. Sound familiar?

I love the Hebrew language. In ancient Hebrew, every letter is both a sound and a picture. The letters in each word combine to paint a word picture that describes the meaning. There are times when the meaning of the word has a clear meaning for us today. I believe that is true with the word for *unity*.

Frank Seekins, a good friend of mine, conducts seminars on Hebrew words and their meanings. Frank helps us here to discover the real meaning of unity as described in the Hebrew language.

The Hebrew word for unity is *echad* and means "strongly fence the door." So from the word picture, unity comes when we strongly fence the door. What does that mean? Frank gives this perspective, "Imagine that you were in a movie theater and you saw a fire starting down in the front of the theater. What are you going to do? If you are like me, you are going to get out fast! But suppose the doors to the theater are locked and there is no way to leave. What are you going to do now? You will have to put out the fire!

"When faced with a choice between the fire and the door, we will take the door. But when the door is locked, we deal with the fire. Unity is found in this simple analogy.

Every relationship is tested in times of trouble.

If we leave a door open, we will not have to confront the fire, and when the fire gets bad enough we have an excuse to leave."

That's a challenging thought. What if we were committed to our nation, employer, church, spouse, etc., with this perspective? I'm not talking about extremely abusive relationships, but far too many relationships are broken because we want to take the easy way out. We never learn to deal with the fire! We just run from one burning theater to another.

Too many Christians run from one church to another, too many employees run from one job to another, too many people run from one relationship to another. Just think about how entire nations and cities could be transformed if we worked out differences rather than becoming polarized over differences.

The key to unity is to first to understand how unity works, then commit to the process of unity. Only you can prevent theater fires!

....

Behold how good and pleasant it is for brethren to dwell together in unity! (Psalm 133:1 NKJV)

84

Dual Citizenship—
Both Tribe and Nation

Criticisms of the community toward the church could be summarized in the following questions, "Why can't churches get along?" "Where is the unity that you should be demonstrating?" "Why are there so many different churches?" Sound familiar? There seems to be more division in the church than unity. That creates a bad public relations image within the surrounding communities—made up of the people the church was sent to serve.

The reason for diverse types of churches goes all the way back to how God designed Israel. He designed Israel to have both a tribal identity and a national identity. There were 12 tribes that comprised the nation of Israel. Each tribe had a unique purpose and calling. The tribe of Judah was a tribe of praise, while the tribe of Joseph was a tribe whose influence went to the nations. The tribe of Levi consisted of specialized temple priests, whereas the tribe of Issachar had experts who saw what God wanted done at various times in history. Each had a unique purpose.

Each tribe had an emphasis or assignment by God. However, each tribe was incomplete without the others. When the tribes came together in unity, they became a nation. A nation is much stronger than a tribe, and much more complete! Tribes are the parts, a nation is the whole! It's like a recipe.

Tribes are the different ingredients that make a cake, the nation is the cake.

This is not a concept that we are unfamiliar with. In fact, our nation, the *United* States of America, was designed on the biblical concept of dual citizenship, both tribe and nation. I am a resident of Arizona living in America. I am a Zonie as well as an American. Arizona has provincial issues that are best handled tribally or locally. However, that doesn't mean that Arizona is not part of America. Tribes tend to focus on the XYZ's whereas nations focus on the ABC's.

In the church arena, each denomination or church movement is a tribe, not the nation. The Presbyterians, Methodists, Calvary Churches, Vineyards, and the like are tribes, not nations. The problem is that churches and denominations tend to think they are the nation! I call this spiritual tribalism—when a tribe thinks it's the nation. Consequently, they project their values on to all the other tribes saying, "If you don't do it or believe in it the way we do, you are wrong!" The result—Christ comes across as divided to the community. In reality, they are not wrong, there are just way too many power struggles going on within the tribes.

Just as the United States has a Constitution that focuses on the foundations of the country, the church has a document that defines Christianity—the Apostle's Creed. Most anything outside of what is in this creed are tribal issues, not national issues.

....

God designed both tribe *and* nation.

85

Parable of the Spoons

Someone recently e-mailed the following to me:

The Parable of the Spoons

A holy man was having a conversation with the Lord one day and said, "Lord, I would like to know what Heaven and hell are like."

The Lord led the holy man to two doors. He opened one of the doors and the holy man looked in. In the middle of the room was a large round table. In the middle of the table was a large pot of stew which smelled delicious and made the holy man's mouth water.

The people sitting around the table were thin and sickly. They appeared to be famished. They were holding spoons with very long handles and each found it possible to reach into the pot of stew and take a spoonful, but because the handle was longer than their arms, they could not get the spoons back into their mouths. The holy man shuddered at the sight of their misery and suffering.

The Lord said, "You have seen hell."

They went to the next room and opened the door. It was exactly the same as the first. There was the large round table with the large pot of stew which made the holy man's mouth water. The people were equipped with the same long-handled spoons, but here the people were well nourished and plump, laughing, and talking.

The holy man said, "I don't understand."

"It is simple," said the Lord. "It requires but one skill. You see, they have learned to feed each other, while the greedy think only of themselves."

Sooner or later, preferably sooner, we learn that we are interdependent, especially in the context of our relationships and community.

Agreement and cooperation are prerequisites to a healthy, productive life.

To many, cooperation and negotiation are the equivalent to compromise. I'm not talking about compromise. I'm talking about wisdom.

Wisdom requires maturity. Maturity has core values but also knows what fights are worth fighting and which are not. The return is not worth the investment. Have you discovered that with your spouse? If not, you will!

Using wisdom, 90 percent of the time we could negotiate rather than separate or isolate. That's what I like about strategic alliances and mutual collaborations. While different, we can work together for a common cause. People who serve don't think less of themselves, they think of themselves less. Don't use what God has given you as a means to an ego-driven end. Even if you win the rat race, you are still a rat!

The real lesson from the Parable of the Spoons—help others and you will thrive, not just survive!

∙∙

People who serve don't think less of themselves,
they think of themselves less.

86

Attitude Determines Altitude

One of the challenges we all face is the challenge of attitude. Is your attitude and outlook nose down or nose up? Are you "never better" or "never worse"? Is the glass half-full or half-empty? Do you more often sing, "Raindrops Keep Falling On My Head," "Make the World Go Away," or "Oh, What a Beautiful Morning"?

Don't get me wrong. Tough things do happen. No one sings, "Oh, What a Beautiful Morning" every day. However, I think most of us would admit that our quality of life is better when our attitude toward life is more positive than negative.

Webster defines *attitude* as "a mental position or feeling with regard to an object...an inward feeling expressed by behavior."

Our attitude drives our behavior.

I recently found a great description of attitude. "It is the 'advance man' of our true selves. Its roots are inward, but its fruit is outward. It is our best friend or our worst enemy. It is more honest and consistent than our words. It is an outward look based on past experiences. It is the thing which draws people to us or repels them. It is never content until it is expressed. It is the librarian of our past. It is the speaker of our present. It is the prophet of our future."[56]

Ability is what you are capable of. *Motivation* determines what you will do. *Attitude* determines how well you will do it.

Attitude can determine whether we reach our full potential or under-achieve. It's impossible to determine how many jobs have been lost, promotions missed, sales not made, marriages ruined, and potential lost because someone "copped an attitude." A bad attitude lengthens the distance to any goal. Yes, pain does happen. However, how we react to pain is the key to a better quality of life. Pain is inevitable but misery is optional!

The story of the Prodigal Son illustrates two types of sin. The younger son illustrated the sin of the flesh while the older son illustrates the sin of attitude. Even though the older son did everything perfect, his attitude undermined him. Watch that attitude!

···

**A positive attitude will take you higher—
a bad attitude keeps you down.**

87

Your Best Friend
or Worst Enemy

Attitudes drive our behaviors. Someone can be constructive or destructive depending upon attitude—a mental position in regard to something. My job in life is to help people reach their goals, dreams, and their full potential. In order to do that, they need to have the right attitude. Ask any employer, school principal, government official, or your neighbor, "What is the hardest thing you have to deal with?" Generally, the answers are some version of: dealing with someone with a destructive attitude.

A bad attitude can infect, affect, and release problems throughout a crowd, team, family, or church that have the potential to undermine morale and production. When teenagers cop an attitude, the household is in turmoil. However, the converse is also true. A person with a great attitude can increase morale and production. That's the power of attitude.

Many times attitude is the difference between success and failure. The Stanford Research Institute reports that the money you make is determined by the following formula. One's product knowledge, ability and IQ skills were 12.5 percent of wage determination criteria. One's ability to deal with people, attitude, and outlook on life were 87.5 percent of the wage determination criteria.[57] In other words, 87.5 percent attitude plus 12.5 percent ability equals a 100 percent better life!

Now, let me tell you a secret, bad attitude cannot happen in your life without your permission. Victor Frankl, the survivor of a Nazi concentration camp says, "The last of the human freedoms is to choose one's attitude in any given set of circumstances."[58]

We become servants of the choices we make.

Once we choose a bad attitude, we become a servant to the bad attitude. The world doesn't care whether we free ourselves from a bad attitude or not. The world marches on. Adopting a good attitude doesn't change the world so much as it changes us. The change cannot come from others. It comes from us.

Apostle Paul knew this principle. He wrote in his letter to the Philippians, "have this attitude in yourselves which was also in Christ Jesus" (Phil. 2:5). What was that attitude? Selflessness.

••

do not merely look out for your own personal interests, but also for the interests of others. Have this attitude in yourselves which was also in Christ Jesus (Philippians 2:4-5).

88

Jesus Has an Attitude!

Did you know Jesus has an attitude? Paul describes his attitude in Philippians chapter 2:3-8:

Do nothing from selfishness or empty conceit, but with humility of mind regard one another as more important than yourselves; do not merely look out for your own personal interests, but also for the interests of others. Have this attitude in yourselves which was also in Christ Jesus, who, although He existed in the form of God, did not regard equality with God a thing to be grasped, but emptied Himself, taking the form of a bond-servant, and being made in the likeness of men. Being found in appearance as a man, He humbled Himself by becoming obedient to the point of death, even death on a cross.

What created this very positive, "can-do" attitude in Jesus? I think it was four very important attitude determiners. He was selfless, secure, submissive, and obedient. Those four personality traits have the potential to change our lives!

If our attitude toward the world is excellent, we will generally receive excellent results. If we feel so-so about the world, our response from the world will be average. If we feel badly about the world, we will receive negative feedback from life.

Remember the very wise proverb of Solomon, "As a man thinks in his heart, so he is" (Prov. 23:7 NKJV).

Selflessness is a rare commodity in this selfish, self-absorbed world. We are bombarded with a take-care-of-number-1, and it's-all-about-me philosophy of life. Now don't get me wrong. A good, healthy self-image is essential; however, good things taken to extremes can become bad things quickly. Life is about giving *and* taking, not just taking. Searching for significance, acceptance, and love in all the wrong places affects attitude.

As a Christian, you live *from* acceptance, not *for* acceptance. You live *from* significance, not *for* significance. You live *from* being loved, not *for* being loved. That's where Christ lived from, and it turned Him inside out! He lived to serve, not to be served.

Jesus was secure. He knew who he was, and where He was. He could see the big picture. He realized God was for Him, not against Him. He knew His present distress was for His future best.

He didn't blame God for everything. He chose to be instructed rather than offended. He didn't make God in His own image. When things went wrong, He trusted. He knew He would understand later. It wasn't blind faith, but a relationship based upon the integrity of God.

That's how you can be more consistently positive. Our cooperation with God's operation leads to an attitude revelation.

•••

Your current distress may be for your future best!

89

Whistle While You Work

God instituted the three building blocks of effective society in the Garden of Eden— marriage, family, and work. He called us into right relationships and meaningful tasks way back in the first garden. Your family and your job are blessings from the Lord.

To have a job is a blessing. Some of my work is published in various cities in South Africa. In many of those areas, unemployment can be as high as 80 percent. We are most fortunate to live in a country that has jobs in abundance. In 2008, unemployment in the United States hovers around 4 percent.

As a Christian, doing your job well is a way of serving and honoring both your employer and the Lord. As a Christian, your job is more than a job. It's an opportunity to demonstrate what a productive, effective, well-mannered employee looks like. You serve God by serving your employer in an excellent way—even some of those "problem" employers.

The Bible says, "...in all things obey those who are your masters on earth, not with external service, as those who merely please men, but with sincerity of heart, fearing [respecting] the Lord. Whatever you do, do your work heartily, as for the Lord rather than for men, knowing that from the Lord you will receive the reward of the inheritance. It is the Lord Christ whom you serve (Col. 3:22-24).

Now that's different! Don't just survive at work, *thrive* at work. Don't just get by, do your work and then some!

Excel, raise the standard, and make both your employer and God happy.

Why not redefine being an employee? I'm not talking about the employer who asks you to be immoral, unethical, or illegal. In that case, leave or report it to the "higher ups" in the company. But until you leave your present employer, serve that employer with gusto! It most likely will give you favor with your employer and the Lord. That's a good thing!

A manager of a large company summarizes what I'm saying in his version of Psalm 23 for work.

"The Lord is my real boss and I shall not want. He gives me peace when chaos is all around me. He gently reminds me to pray and do all things without murmuring and complaining. He reminds me that He is my source and not my job. He restores my sanity everyday and guides my decisions that I might honor Him in all that I do. Even though I face absurd amounts of e-mails, system crashes, unrealistic deadlines, budget cutbacks, gossiping co-workers, discriminating supervisors, and an aging body that doesn't cooperate every morning, I still will not stop, for He is with me. His presence, His peace, and His power will see me through. He raises me up, even when they fail to promote me. He claims me as His own, even when the company threatens to let me go. His faithfulness and love is better than any bonus check. His retirement plan beats every 401K there is. And, when it's all said and done, I'll be working for Him a whole lot longer and for that, I bless His name!"[59]

You see, whether you love your job or hate your job, you can whistle while you work when your employer is the Lord!

••

Whistle while you work—and smile!

90

The King of Fruits

For two weeks my 16-year-old son Jon and I were in Singapore. I was speaking in churches in this mega-engine of commerce. The joke in Singapore is all they do is make money, shop, and eat. I know what you are thinking, sounds good, huh?

This paradise was perfect for Jon, because he is a fruit lover. Our hosts introduced him to all of the tropical fruit of Singapore. Jon loved it. He was willing to try any fruit given to him. Frankly, there was some weird fruit there.

Jon tried dragon fruit, guava, star fruit, snake skin fruit (don't ask), soursop (sounds delicious), dugong, water apples, hami melon, longan (dragon eye fruit, oh joy), persimmon, mango-stein, jack fruit, finger banana's, and other fruit I can't begin to pronounce.

Jon enjoyed each fruit. However, he didn't know about the King of the Fruits—durian.

Like a lamb led to the slaughter, our hosts set him up for a taste of durian which is the talk of the entire country.

For one thing, you smell durian before you see durian. It smells terrible, at least to most people. I remember boarding a jet in India and a passenger brought a durian onboard, placing it in the overhead compartment. As I recall, both the durian and the passenger were removed from the plane. None too soon I might add.

Durian is mossy green in color, about the size of a rugby football. It has spikes on it that should warn even the most innocent potential partaker. Our hosts thought that durian was smooth before the fall of man.

As you open the durian, that which you already smell on the outside increases exponentially. Let's just say Clark Kent turns into Superman. As Jon prepared to take a bite of durian, everything in him was crying "Danger Will Robinson!" The icy-looking inside tasted like "egg yokes" to Jon. He escaped alive, living another day to enjoy more user-friendly fruit.

To most Singaporeans, the durian is the King of the Fruits. They have durian ice cream, pancakes, moon cakes, muffins, puffs, and the like. But the true test was to eat the durian by itself. "After you get used to it, you love it," said our Asian hosts.

There's a lesson in that fruit story. Sometimes things happen to people that are like durians. However, once they get past the initial shock, they see how God used it to make them better, wiser, or more mature. Who knows, they might even like their durian someday after they see how God used it in their lives. My host in Singapore says, "Taste and see that the Lord is good, even in those durian times!"

....

O taste and see that the Lord is good; How blessed is the man who takes refuge in Him! (Psalm 34:8)

91

Speaking for Responsibility

One of the best stories I have ever heard about taking personal responsi-bility comes from author John Maxwell in his book *Developing the Leader Within You*. Fasten your seat belts.

The sales manager of a dog food company asked his sales people how they liked the company's new advertising program.

"Great! The best in the business," the sales people responded.

"How do you like our new label and package?"

"Great. The best in the business," the sales people responded.

"How do you like our sales force?" They were the sales force. They had to admit they were very good.

"OK, then," said the manager, "so we've got the best label, and the best advertising program being sold by the best sales force in the business. Tell me why we are in 17th place in the dog food business?"

Finally someone said, "It's those lousy dogs. They won't eat the stuff!"[60]

Taking responsibility is a matter of choice. Now of course, there are real victims. There are people through no fault of their own have had terrible things happen to them—a car accident caused by someone else, assaults, and so forth. But I'm writing about people who choose to be in denial about their situation. They blame society, someone or something else, the past, or just outright lie to hide the real issue. They feel entitled to do so. Their life's mantra seems to be: if at first you don't succeed, destroy all the evidence that you tried.

Now, we all come very naturally to this stance on life. After the fall in the Garden of Eden, Adam blamed God for his shortcomings. His statement to God, after God saw a few apples missing from the tree, was, "the women you gave me made me do it!" Of course, Eve blamed it on the snake. Their oldest son, Cain, killed their youngest son, Abel, because Cain could not take responsibility for his own actions.

Our propensity to blame shift and not take personal responsibility came from the first man and woman. We have had lots of time to perfect it. "It's those lousy dogs. They won't eat the stuff!" Denial is not a river in Egypt, it's something breeding inside us! The philosophy of everything is someone else's fault and excuse is the morphine of our time.

As long as we fix the blame, we can't fix the problem.

The problem is the more we play the victim when we aren't, the more it becomes a part of our lifestyle. It colors our perspective and causes us to underachieve.

I see the potential in people almost to a fault. I see what people can be. I believe for the best in people. But a blame mentality will never get them there. Being all that we can be starts with, "Lord, I have a problem—it's me!"

•••

**Adam blamed God, Eve blamed Adam,
and the snake didn't have a leg to stand on!**

92

Responding to Responsibility

The teenager lost a contact lens while playing basketball in his driveway. After a fruitless search, he went inside and told his mother the lens was nowhere to be found. Undaunted, she went outside and in a few minutes, returned with the lens in her hand.

"How did you manage to find it, Mom?" the teenager asked.

"We weren't looking for the same thing," she replied. "You were looking for a small piece of plastic. I was looking for $150!"

Many people who are struggling with taking responsibility are stuck in a warped mindset. Let's explore how to get unstuck from blame shifting and other coping mechanisms that take people farther away from where they want to be and where God wants them to be.

As I mentioned previously, I'm not talking about true victims. I'm talking about those who take on a mindset of being the perpetual victim. People who see the glass half empty are many times the ones draining the water away. Their philosophy of life is the hardness of the butter is proportional to the softness of the bread. The colder the x-ray table, the more of your body is required to be on it.

I've heard it said that, "The trials of life will either wear you down or polish you up, depending on what you are made of." I'm not trying to lay a guilt trip on anyone. I'm trying to say that how we respond to what has happened to us, or what we think happened to us, is the main issue. As you've

217

read previously, the Bible says in Proverbs 23:7, "For as a man thinks within himself, so he is." That goes for women too.

Notice the word *respond*.

Responsibility is responding to God's ability to help you *through* what you have gone through!

Being responsible is to realize our choices are significant—what we do affects who we are and where we will end up. Our future is flexible. Our life is like a river. We can allow ourselves to go with the flow and see where various currents take us, but we do have control enough to paddle to the bank or move upstream.

An awareness of the role we play in our own lives is essential if we are to move away from the victim mentality. If it's going to be, it starts with me—with God's help.

....

**Your future is flexible—
don't restrict it with self-defeating thoughts.**

93

Watch Your Thoughts, They Become...

While flying back to the United States from South Africa I found a word treasure in the *SkyMall* magazine. A poster was for sale that said the following quote by Frank Outlaw:

Watch Your Thoughts, They Become Words

Watch Your Words, They Become Actions

Watch Your Actions, They Become Habits

Watch Your Habits, They Become Character

Watch Your Character, It Becomes Your Destiny!

This flow of concept can be used in our lives either positively or negatively. We can either build ourselves up or tear ourselves down depending on how we think of ourselves, others, our circumstances, or our community.

Your thoughts eventually determine your destiny. There is a process in us that starts in thought, moves to words, and then expresses itself in actions. I call it thinking, speaking, doing—moving from head, to heart, to feet. Everything starts with thoughts and ideas. Everything starts with how you think about something. There is a battle for the mind both internally and externally, privately, or publicly. Each of us has the personal responsibility of minding our mind. The fulfillment of your purpose and destiny depend on it!

Every act reported in the public newspaper started with a private thought.

Like seeds grow into plants, thoughts grow into actions. Thinking affects your speech, your speech affects your behavior, your behavior affects your success in life. Those who can mind their mind, generally go higher and further in life. Your thoughts can make you or break you.

I once counseled a very bitter person whose life was constantly filled with calamity and pathos. While trying to help her, she made one of the most insightful destiny-determining statements I have ever heard. As we were talking about broken relationships she said, "Whether right or wrong, I didn't get what I wanted!" Ouch, I feel her pain even as I'm writing this. Remember, as a person thinks in their heart, so they become—positively or negatively.

What you and I think about life, our relationships, jobs, communities, and ourselves can determine our destiny. The Bible addresses this principle in Romans 12:1-3. I'll paraphrase: don't be conformed to the world's way of thinking, be transformed by the renewing of your mind so you can receive God's destiny for you; learn to think so as to have sound judgment.

A new way of thinking is more than emotion based or philosophy biased. Sound judgment is a way of thinking that focuses on the big picture, sees God's perspective, and looks ahead to where your thoughts are taking you and how they could influence your life positively or negatively.

● ●

**Sound judgment and a renewed mind are the rewards
for reading the Bible. Try it, you'll like it!**

94

A Dog's Purpose

Every once and awhile we read or learn something that cleans up the clutter of our complicated lives. These moments refocus us and send us on the way again with a fresh burst of truth, energizing us and propelling us forward. Usually for me, it is when something profound has been said or illustrated in a very simple way. Something unexpected, something that is very wise, illustrated in a very simple way. God loves to do that. He makes wise the simple.

Here's a story that has been circulating on the Internet that struck me that way. It's about a dog's purpose and a 4-year-old boy.

Being a veterinarian, I had been called to examine a 10-year-old Irish Wolfhound named Belker. The dog's owners and their little boy, Shane, were all very attached to Belker, and were hoping for a miracle. I examined Belker and found he was dying of cancer. I told the family that we could not do anything about Belker and offered to perform the euthanasia procedure for the old dog in their home.

As we made the arrangements, the parents thought it might be good for Shane to observe the procedure. They thought Shane might learn something from the experience. The next day, I felt that familiar catch in my throat as Belker's family surrounded him and I prepared for the procedure. Shane seemed so calm, petting the dog for the last time, that I wondered if he understood what was going on. Within a few minutes, Belker slipped peacefully away.

The little boy seemed to accept Belker's transition without any confusion or difficulty. We sat together for a while after Belker's death, wondering about the sad fact that dogs lives are shorter than human lives. Shane, who had been listening quietly, piped up and said,

"I know why!"

Startled, we all turned to him. What came out of his mouth stunned me. I never heard a more comforting explanation.

The 4-year-old said, "People are born so that they can learn how to live a good life, like loving everybody all the time and being nice, right? Well, dogs already know how to do that so they don't have to stay as long!"

That's good reasoning from a 4-year-old. Now, all we have to do is apply it to our lives. Doggone it, that will be a little harder!

· ·

**Live simply, love generously, care deeply, speak kindly,
and leave the rest to God.**

95

Critical Analysis?

I hate to say it, but we are becoming a society of analysts. We are becoming more like spectators than participants. We tend to analyze, criticize, categorize, and marginalize. We tend to think we are experts at everything. Someone once said,

"One good thing about being wrong is the joy it brings to others." Hello?

I recently received an e-mail called, Management Lesson.

An eagle was sitting in a tree, resting, doing nothing. A small rabbit saw the eagle and asked him, "Can I also sit like you and do nothing?"

The eagle answered, "Sure, why not?"

So, the rabbit sat on the ground below the eagle and rested. All of a sudden, a fox appeared, jumped on the rabbit and ate it.

The management lesson: To be sitting and doing nothing, you must be sitting very, very high up.[61]

Being a critic seems fine when you're the one criticizing, but how about when you are the one being criticized? How about when you are the player and not the spectator? How about when you are on the field, not in the stands? Different story, huh?

That is what Jesus was dealing with in His time. Jesus taught people to analyze sensitively. Jesus knew the debilitating power of destructive criticism. He also knew the power of constructive criticism when done with a right attitude. He knows that too many of us are desperate to be the experts of everything. He taught people to look at themselves first before they look at others. He was aware that if you sow criticism, you will reap criticism. His expert analysis, "Do not judge, lest you be judged by others" (Matt. 7:1). He also said, "You hypocrite, first take the log out of your own eye, and *then* you will see clearly enough to take the speck out of your brother's eye" (Matt. 7:5).

It's one small step from being critical about life to becoming cynical. It's one small step from being critical of people to becoming cynical. It's one small step from moving from a judge to holding a grudge!

Isn't it wonderful that Jesus came with grace *and* truth. Two times in the Gospel of John, John makes sure that we get the sequence right (see John 1:14,17). Grace, then truth! Truth without grace is a recipe for cynicism and logs in your eye! I'm not saying that we shouldn't fix the problem. However, before we try to fix the problem we ought to fix our approach. Is it constructive or destructive? Is it personal? Is it redemptive?

....

I have to remind myself all the time,
"Quit griping about the world... if it was perfect, I wouldn't belong in it!"

96

The Value of Vision

I ministered in Malaysia a few years ago. It was hot, rainy, and humid. But Malaysia is one of those countries that grows on you. The longer I was there, the more I liked it. Malaysia is a country full of vision and hope. I ministered in the capital city of Kuala Lumpur where two of the tallest buildings in the world are located. I liked the people, they have vision!

With all the things that are going on in the world today, it's easy to lose vision. And yet, in times like these, vision is exactly what we need to keep us going. An optimist thinks that this is the best possible world. A pessimist fears that this is true! Don't give in to the urge to give up. In just two days, tomorrow will be yesterday.

Helen Keller, a woman who lost her sight and hearing at a young age, was asked, "What could possibly be worse than being blind?"

Her reply, "Having sight without vision."[62]

Now, there's a statement for you. Many have sight but cannot see the endless possibilities surrounding them. Having a vision will keep you going when circumstances, events, and trouble start to surround you. You must have a reason for being. You must have a goal. You must have forward motion. Vision is life. Vision enables you to go the extra mile.

Vision is a compelling picture of a preferable future that motivates you to perform. Vision is catalytic. It gets your motor running so you can head out on the highway. Vision is motivational in its essence.

Visionaries are people who see a picture of what they want and can communicate that vision in a way that inspires, motivates, and activates themselves and/or people toward a purpose. They have the ability to see the end from the beginning. Vision comes from having a purpose. Vision motivates you toward that purpose.

The Bible has much to say and reveal to you about vision, for instance, "Where there is no vision, the people are unrestrained..." (Prov. 29:18). That means they are emotionally and mentally thrown about like a boat on a stormy sea. Whatever happens, all they can do is react to what is going on in their life.

I want to encourage you to dream again. My friend's wife, when he is disheartened, says to him,

"Go to God and dream again!"

She knows his signs of obscure vision. More advice—read the Bible and learn about the power of vision. Read about visionaries like Abraham, Joshua, Joseph, Deborah, Esther, Daniel, Paul, and John. All of these people faced tough times much harder than ours today.

....

Never be afraid to try something new.
Remember, amateurs built the ark, professionals built the Titanic!

97

Want to Go Up? Write It Down?

An elderly couple was worried because they kept forgetting things. The doctor assured them that there was nothing seriously wrong except old age. He suggested they carry a notebook and write things down so they wouldn't forget.

Several days later, the man got up from his chair in the living room to go to the kitchen. His wife said, "Dear, get me a bowl of ice cream while you're up."

"OK," he said.

"…and put some chocolate syrup on it and a few cherries on it, too," she added. "You better write all that down."

"I won't forget," he said.

Twenty minutes later he came back into the room and handed her a plate of scrambled eggs and bacon. She glared at him.

"Now, I told you to write it down! I knew you would forget!"

"What did I forget?" he asked.

"My toast!" she said.[63]

To those who might be dissatisfied with old age and would like to go back youthful times, remember Algebra! Enough said.

Let's talk about vision. Vision is a compelling picture of a preferable future that motivates one to perform. The prophet Habakkuk in the Bible knew the process of vision. First, you have to see the vision, then write down the vision for yourself and others, and then *do* the vision. See the vision, write the vision, tell the vision, and then, do the vision. Most are good at the tel-a-vision part but don't know how to do-a-vision.

Where does the successful completion of a creative enterprise start? In the write-a-vision part. Writing the vision turns an idea into something you and others can read and understand. In Habakkuk 2:2 the Bible says, "Then the Lord answered me and said, 'Record the vision and inscribe it on tablets, that the one who reads it may run.'" You see, writing down a vision is necessary for communicating it to others!

Just think of how many good ideas have been lost because the ideas were not written down.

You can move from dream to done just by having a notepad next to your bed each night.

If you are like me, you hate it when you try and remember that wonderful idea that you had in the middle of the night. I've lost more ideas that way! Sound familiar?

Also, writing the vision down can help you when considering the cost of the vision as well as guide you in the process of making the vision a reality. Jesus says in Luke 14:28-30 in The Message translation, "Is there anyone here who, planning to build a new house, doesn't first sit down and figure the cost so you'll know if you can complete it? If you only get the foundation laid and then run out of money, you're going to look pretty foolish. Everyone passing by will poke fun at you: 'He started something he couldn't finish.'"

<hr/>

Write it down—that way you'll get toast with your eggs!

98

The $10 Challenge

"I hate being late," my friend lamented. "It has been a problem for me all my life."

"Do you really want to change that?" I asked.

"Yes, I do," was the response.

"OK. Every time you are late to work or anywhere else where you have committed to be at a particular time, you must give me $25."

"No way!" my friend responded. "I would go broke! But I will do $10."

"All right, $10 it is. It has to be a large enough amount of money for it to hurt your pocketbook."

"Believe me, that will hurt," my friend said.

About a month later my friend found great motivation to be on time. In the first week, I got $10 from my friend. The next week $20. The third week nothing. By the fifth week, my friend had changed a lifelong habit that had hindered her. In order for my friend not to be resentful of me for the money she had given, we put it in a jar to be given to a Christian cause. This ensured my motive was only for her best interest.

Great story, huh? Os Hillman of Marketplace Leaders[64] wrote that story.

What is the principle at work in that story? Until pain exceeds fear there will be no change. The cost has to exceed the comfort of tolerating the unacceptable. Most of us like no pain, no pain! You can't change what you can tolerate. Sometimes accountability or crisis is needed to kill that dragon of a besetting habit. Most people, sooner or later, discover there are consequences tomorrow for what they do today. Payday, someday!

I remember when I was learning how to fly an airplane. At first, I was overwhelmed by all the instruments to watch, the control towers instructions, bringing up the landing gear, adjusting the propeller speed, and flying the plane. However, as I began to fly the plane more and more, these very intentional actions became automatic. I didn't even have to think about it anymore.

I had discovered the power of habit.

Just like the "$10 lady"!

The Bible says, "...For by what a man is overcome, by this he is enslaved" (2 Peter 2:19).

So, here is the $10 challenge for you. What are the habits that keep you from becoming all that God wants you to become? Do you desire change enough to be accountable in a way that costs you something when you fail? Ask a friend, perhaps a counselor, to hold you accountable in an area that needs change. It could be the cheapest $10, the most expensive $10, the most invaluable $10 you have ever spent in your life.

· ·

**Think of a habit today and if it is holding you back...
choose to break it!**

99

Keep Your Hope!

Dogs live in a state of perpetual hope. I love that about dogs. They live in constant expectation of future good. Our family dog's name is Squirt. She's one of those white, curly haired, high-impact, low-maintenance type of dogs. At the beginning of any mealtime, she camps out under the kitchen table hoping to catch a tidbit of any kind of human food. She is not affected by our family's irregular mealtime lifestyle, and it matters not to her if she doesn't get rewarded for her efforts—she lives in a state of perpetual hope. Her hope floats no matter what.

Not so with us humans. Perhaps we are more like cats. We need to see and experience hopeful events at more frequent intervals.

Have you noticed that hope is getting harder to find in our world? Wars, relationship problems, personal problems, politics, and a myriad of other issues weigh on us like a wet, green, Army blanket. National media's emphasis on presenting tragedies perpetuates our woe-is-me outlook of life, and add to that a doctor's bad report, another profit-losing year at work, or a broken relationship, and hope disappears like the retractable point on a ballpoint pen. I've been there, and it's no fun.

People need to have hope to maintain physical and emotional health. Hope is the expectation of future good. Hope is comfort, expectation, confidence, and trust all wrapped up in one gift from God.

Hope provides the outlook and strength to go forward.

Without hope, we cannot have faith, for faith is the assurance of things hoped for (Heb. 11:1). Without hope, people give up on themselves and sometimes life itself. The Bible says in Proverbs 13:12 that, "hope deferred makes the heart sick...." That's true! Where there is no hope for the future, there is no power for the present. That's why keeping your hope alive is so important.

Now for some perspective. There is always hope. Author Mike Murdock says there are no hopeless situations, only people who have grown hopeless about the situations. In the Bible, every miracle started with a problem. If you have a problem, you are a candidate for a miracle. Your hope *can* float!

Hoping in hope won't make things much better. However, hoping in God can! The object of our hope is crucial. In Romans 15:13, God is called the "God of hope." So go to the Source of hope. Romans 15:13 goes on to say that, "the God of hope [will] fill you will all joy and peace in believing, so that you will abound in hope by the power of the Holy Spirit."

Oh by the way, Squirt is still under the kitchen table.

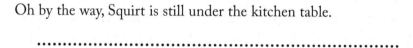

**Hope springs eternal...
allow it to keep your spirit refreshed!**

100

Two Powerful Words

Two friends meet in the street. The one man looked rather forlorn and sad. The other asked, "Hey, how come you look like the whole world caved in?"

The sad fellow said, "Let me tell you. Three weeks ago, an uncle died and left me ten thousand dollars."

"I'm sorry to hear about the death, but a bit of good luck for you, eh?"

"Hold on, I'm just getting started. Two weeks ago, a cousin I never knew kicked the bucket and left me twenty thousand dollars, free and clear."

"Well, you can't be disappointed with that!"

"But, last week my grandfather passed away. I inherited almost one hundred thousand dollars."

"Incredible…so how come you look so glum?"

"Well, this week—nothing!"

Now that's gratitude?

We Americans traditionally give thanks one day every November—but what if we cultivated an attitude of gratitude *every* day of the year? Gratitude keeps things in the right perspective. In a Peanuts cartoon, Charlie Brown is giving Snoopy dog food for his Thanksgiving Day dinner. Snoopy stares at the bowl and talks to himself, *How about that? Everyone is eating turkey today, but just because I'm a dog, I get dog food.* He then trots away and positions himself on top of his doghouse and concludes, *Of course, it could have been much worse, I could have been born a turkey.*

Wouldn't you agree our hurried, hassled, hot-tempered, have-it-my-way world leads us away from a lifestyle of thanksgiving? Gratitude keeps us from the destructiveness of bitterness. The Bible says, "Make sure no one gets left out of God's generosity. Keep a sharp eye out for weeds of bitter discontent" (Heb. 12:15 TM).

An attitude of gratitude permeates the atmosphere with positive energy.

Bitterness and ungratefulness does the opposite.

Every experience in life can make you bitter or better—it is your choice. Don't let bitterness over something that someone has said or done prevent you from rising above the situation. God can turn your greatest tragedy into your greatest triumph. When you can't see God's hand, trust in His character.

Gratitude gives you a confident assurance about the future. A friend promised his 8-year-old son, Bobby, that he would take him fishing on Saturday. The boy waited eagerly for the day to arrive, but rain spoiled their plans. Bobby grumbled all morning, moping about the house. By 3 o'clock in the afternoon, the rain ended and they went fishing. They caught a boatload of fish. At supper, Bobby's mother asked him to say grace. Bobby did so and concluded his prayer with, "And, Lord, if I sounded grumpy earlier in the day, it was because I couldn't see far enough ahead. Thank you for the fish."

Don't forget two very powerful words to say every day of your life: "Thank you."

• •

How far ahead are you looking?

Conclusion

The Power of One Decision

Saying thank you is a great way to end up the days of our life here on earth, but what about Heaven? If you are ready to think God is a reality, then you can believe that there is life after death! And the way to get into heaven is through His Son Jesus. We have talked about Him all through this book. He is wisdom and the way to God.

Look at what God says in The Message version of the Bible in Romans 10:9-10.

> …The word that saves us is right here, as near as the tongue in your mouth, as close as the heart in your chest. It's the word of faith that welcomes God to go to work and set things right for us. This is the core of our preaching. Say the welcoming word to God—"Jesus is my Master"—embracing, body and soul, God's work of doing in us what He did in raising Jesus from the dead. That's it. You're not "doing" anything; you're simply calling out to God, trusting Him to do it for you. That's salvation. With your whole being you embrace God setting things right, and then you say it, right out loud: "God has set everything right between Him and me."

There is a prayer that you can pray that embraces what these Bible verses say. I prayed it when I was 24 years old back in March 1974 on a snowmobile at 3:00AM in Pinetop, Arizona. I've never been the same since. I've found that God is reliable. I've found that God is who He says He is. I've found that God does what He says He will do. I've never turned back nor do I want

235

to turn back. I found a new life. It's not weird, all religious stuff! My life is just the way I know you would like yours to be—normal but supernatural. Look over the prayer that follows and, if you are ready, go ahead and pray it if it expresses what you want God to do for you. No pressure, it's just God and you. Here's the prayer.

God...I receive your Son Jesus into my heart. Even though I don't understand it all, I say by the faith that I have, Jesus is Lord, and I believe that God raising Him from the dead is what He is going to do for me. Thank you for making things right between me and You. I thank You that I have a new start. Receive me Lord. Amen.

If you prayed that prayer and meant it, welcome to a bigger world! Welcome to what God created you for. Welcome, to the family of God. God has lit the candle of your life and you are fully completed, already producing the light that God has called you to. You have discovered the power of one decision.

Now for the rest of you, I hope that this book has touched you in many areas. My sincere desire is that you could say after reading this book, "Ed, you have touched me and I have grown!" I hope I have moved you from unaware to aware, unconcerned to concerned, or uninterested to interest in God. I hope that you are closer to God now than when you started reading this book. I hope your heart and mind have been opened to God. That would be wonderful! Don't forget, the power of one decision is ready when you are.

—Ed Delph

Endnotes

1. *The Word for Today* is a devotional written by Bob and Debby Gass with Ruth Gass Halliday, published by United Christian Broadcasters, www.ucb.co.uk.

2. Laurie Beth Jones, *Teach Your Team to Fish* (NY: Crown Business, 2002).

3. Mike Murdock, *Wisdom for Crisis Times* (Tulsa, OK: Honor Books, 1994).

4. Mike Murdock, *The One-Minute Businessman's Devotional* (Tulsa, OK: Honor Books, 1994).

5. Zig Ziglar, *Life Lifters* (Nashville, TN: Broadman & Holman Publishers, 2003).

6. Dwight Thompson, *Power Principles for Power Living* (Houston, TX: Cornerstone Publications, 1991).

7. http://www.cybersalt.org/cleanlaugh/archive/3rdexplanation.htm.

8. brainyquote.com.

9. www.snopes.com/politics/religion/godpoll.asp.

10. The Barna Update, September 24, 2007.

11. Zig Ziglar, *Life Lifters* (Nashville, TN: Broadman & Holman Publishers, 2003), 91.

12. Story taken from www.story-lovers.com.

13. www.quoteworld.com.

14. www.writeathome.wordpress.com.

15. www.realjokes.net.

16. www.banderacountycourier.com.

17. www.brainyquote.com.

18. www.brainyquote.com.

19. www.twainquotes.com.

20. http://www.nyc-architecture.com/GON/GON005.htm, accessed March 10, 2008.

21. Stan Toler, *Minute Motivators for Leaders* (Honor Books or Choice Books), 138.

22. Ziglar, *Life Lifters*, 3.

23. www.cybersalt.com.

24. www.emmitsburg.net/humor.

25. www.characterfirst.com or The Character Training Institute.

26. www.dial-a-joke.com

27. *The Word For Today*, Winter 2006-2007, page 21; www.ubc.co.uk.

28. Toler, *Minute Motivators For Leaders*.

29. Quote by Charles H. Spurgeon.

30. www.expeditionportal.com.

31. Mike Murdock, *One-Minute Businessman's Devotional* (Honor Books, 1992), 66.

32. Many quotes and stories have been taken from the book by Warren Weirsbe, *Be Joyful*.

33. John Maxwell, *The Power of Partnership In the Church* (J.Countrymen Publishers, 1999), 121.

34. www.history.com; copyright 2005 by Jerry Wilson. Used by permission.

35. The First Parent; www.bibleshack.com.

36. www.dennydavis.net.

37. www.cybersalt.com.

38. www.louisvilleemmanaus.com.

39. Dwight Thompson, *Power Principles for Power Living* (Cornerstone Publications, 1991), 43.

40. www.DNRonline.com.

41. www.cybersalt.com.

42. www.cybersalt.com.

43. www.uadmin.blogspot.com.

44. www.brainyquote.com.

45. www.cybersalt.com.

46. www.boreme.com.

47. *The Word for Today*, Winter 2006-07.

48. Murdock, 93.

49. www.cybersalt.com.

50. www.byfaithonly.com.

51. Stan Toler, *You May Be a Preacher If...* (Albury Publishing, 1996).

52. Simon and Garfunkel, "I Am a Rock," *Best of Simon and Garfunkel*; http://www.lyricsdepot.com/simon-and-garfunkel/i-am-a-rock.html.

53. www.netfunny.com.

54. www.i-cop.org.

55. *Peter Lowe's Success Yearbook* (1998), 24.

56. www.christiansoliderscross.com.

57. John Maxwell, *The Winning Attitude* (Here's Life Publishers, 1991).

58. Ibid.

59. Ibid.

60. John Maxwell, *Developing the Leader Within You* (New York: Thomas Nelson, 2005).

61. www.cybersalt.com.

62. www.brainyquote.com.

63. www.cybersalt.com.

64. Visit www.marketplaceleaders.org.

Inspirations

_____

_____

_____

_____

_____

_____

_____

_____

_____

_____

Contact the Author

Ed Delph
Nationstrategy
7145 W. Mariposa Grande Lane
Peoria, Arizona 85383

www.nationstrategy.com
Nationstrategy@cs.com

Other books by Ed Delph

Making Sense of Apostolic Ministry
Church @ Community

Additional copies of this book and other
book titles from DESTINY IMAGE are
available at your local bookstore.

Call toll-free: 1-800-722-6774.

Send a request for a catalog to:

Destiny Image₍ Publishers, Inc.
P.O. Box 310
Shippensburg, PA 17257-0310

*"Speaking to the Purposes of God for This
Generation and for the Generations to Come."*

**For a complete list of our titles,
visit us at www.destinyimage.com.**